YOU
ACH
MORE

LIVE BY DESIGN, NOT BY DEFAULT

YOU CAN ACHIEVE MORE

LIVE BY DESIGN, NOT BY DEFAULT

SHIV KHERA

BLOOMSBURY BUSINESS

LONDON · NEW YORK · OXFORD · NEW DELHI · SYDNEY

BLOOMSBURY BUSINESS
Bloomsbury Publishing Plc
50 Bedford Square, London, WC1B 3DP, UK
1385 Broadway, New York, NY 10018, USA

BLOOMSBURY, BLOOMSBURY BUSINESS and the Diana logo are trademarks
of Bloomsbury Publishing Plc

First published in Great Britain 2018

A catalogue record for this book is available from the British Library.

Library of Congress Cataloging-in-Publication Data
Names: Khera, Shiv, author.
Title: You can achieve more : live by design, not by default / Shiv Khera.
Description: London ; New York, NY : Bloomsbury Business, 2018. |
Includes bibliographical references and index.
Identifiers: LCCN 2018023848 (print) | LCCN 2018025706 (ebook) |
ISBN 9789386950512 (ePUB) | ISBN 9789386950529 (pbk.)
Subjects: LCSH: Success. | Self-realization. | Conduct of life.
Classification: LCC BJ1611.2 (ebook) | LCC BJ1611.2 .K52 2018 (print) |
DDC 158–dc23
LC record available at https://lccn.loc.gov/2018023848

ISBN: PB: 978-9-3869-5052-9
          eBook: 978-9-3869-5051-2

Printed and bound in Great Britain

To find out more about our authors and books visit www.bloomsbury.com and
sign up for our newsletters.

I dedicate this book to…

My Mother for being my North Star
My Wife who is my soulmate
My Children and Grandchildren who are my most precious relationships
And God for His choicest blessings

Contents

Acknowledgements

A ny accomplishment requires the effort of many people and this work is no different. I thank my wife whose patience and support was instrumental in accomplishing this task. I thank my staff whose diligent effort made this publication possible.

Many examples, stories, and anecdotes are a result of a collection from various sources, such as newspapers, magazines, other speakers and seminar participants over the last few decades. Unfortunately, sources were not always noted or available; hence, it became impractical to provide an accurate acknowledgment. Regardless of the source, I wish to express my gratitude to those who may have contributed to this work, even though anonymously. Every effort has been made to give credit where it is due for the material contained herein. If, inadvertently, I have omitted to give credit, future publications will give due credit to those that are brought to the author's attention.

Introduction

ACHIEVE MORE and BECOME UNSTOPPABLE

A person with a positive attitude cannot be stopped. A person with a negative attitude cannot be helped. In other words, a person with a positive attitude is unstoppable. Life is an obstacle course, and many a time we become our own biggest obstacles. People reach **great heights** in life only when they have **great depths of character.**

What Kind of a Book is This?

This book is a road map for a journey to **Achieve More**. It illustrates and clarifies to help find direction in a cluttered environment.

Acquiring facts is **knowledge,** interpreting facts is **understanding,** and the proper application of facts is **wisdom.** An idea dies unless it is acted upon. **The best idea will not work, unless we work the idea.** The objective of this book is to help create an action plan to optimise our potential, or in other words, **ACHIEVE MORE...**

Success does not depend only upon special skills, formal education or superior intelligence. Success is neither a miracle nor a mystery. It is the natural outcome of consistently applying certain principles on an ongoing basis. The difference between success and failure lies in the degree of our commitment to seek and apply these principles.

The principles in this book are universal and eternal. Universal means that they cut across country, culture and religion. Eternal means that they were here before we came and they will be here after we are gone. These principles are simple, but not easy to implement. None of them will work unless they are put into action.

While the messages contained in this book are timeless, due to their relevance, they are desperately needed today more than ever before. In fact, this book covers topics that resonate with every person's life.

When we come to this world, no one is guaranteed success. Gimmicks do not produce positive results. There are many books that teach us how to plan, eat and dress for success, but this book effectively helps in learning not only the principles of success, but also in avoiding expensive mistakes. Diligently practising the principles in this book will help us develop confidence, making life more meaningful and rewarding. Applying these principles requires a lot of self-discipline and commitment. However, once applied, the results are rewarding and gratifying.

The ultimate goal of success is to achieve happiness. After much introspection, I've come to the conclusion that **in order to be happy, we need three things — HEALTH, WEALTH AND GOOD RELATIONSHIPS.**

1. **Health:** People who lack good health, can they be happy? The obvious answer is no. Supposing, you have all the wealth in the world and great relationships too, but don't have good health, can you be happy?
2. **Wealth:** By wealth, here, I mean financial wealth. There are people who believe and make others believe that financial wealth is not important in this world. Of course, it is not the most important of factors, but it is important enough for a peaceful sustenance. Those who say it is not important are either stupid or billionaires. If wealth does not bring happiness, well poverty certainly does not bring it either. I've not seen many poor and destitute people happy.
3. **Good Relationships:** Without good relationships, people feel a void in their lives, which can lead to either insecurity or loneliness. I have never seen a person who has nasty relationships being truly happy. A person could have all the health and wealth in the world, but without good relationships would be emotionally bankrupt.

If any one of the three above goes missing, how can we have happiness? And if anyone can be happy under such circumstances, he is an exception.

If we want to be successful and happy, then we must become students and study the lives of successful people in depth. If we want to be healthy, we must study the principles of good health. If we want to become wealthy, then we must study the principles of acquiring wealth. If we want to have good relationships, we must acquire the principles of good relationships.

Where we will be five years from now will depend on **whether we live by design or by default.**

Most people are looking to live extraordinary lives. To some it may also mean extraordinary income. They need to ask themselves:

1. **Are they extraordinary people?**
2. **Are they willing to work extraordinarily hard?**
3. **Do they have extraordinary commitments?**
4. **Do they have extraordinary relationships?**
5. **Do they have extraordinary integrity?**

At the end of our lives, we do not want to arrive at a destination that makes us feel it wasn't of our choice. If we end up living or doing things we did not want to do, then we've arrived **by default not by design.** We may or may not realise it, but life moves very fast. To avoid regrets towards the end of one's life, one needs to make the right kind of choices to begin with. We need to know when to say yes and when to say no.

Learning to make a living and learning to live are two different things. **This book helps us design a meaningful life**.

Both success and failure have a limited lifespan. Our objective is to sustain success and eliminate failure. One cannot consistently achieve success without preparation. **If we want to stand out, then we need to do something outstanding** or we will get lost in the crowd. This book guides us to **make positive choices and avoid pitfalls.**

How Do I Read This Book?

Please do not rush through this book. Go slow. Think through every page. Step back and think with the acquired knowledge—if we go back in time, would we take the same decisions that we did in the past? Make notes on the side; highlight and mark what appeals to you the most. Divide it into three sections: your goals, the stages in which you plan to reach them, and a timetable within which to achieve them. You should discuss these concepts with someone close to you. By the time you finish this book, your notes will become the foundation on which you can build your new life. Personalise the message from this book to **ACHIEVE MORE.**

Throughout the book, I have used the masculine gender only for the ease in writing.

Start an Action Plan

If there is one universal truth that I would like to pass on to the next generation, it would be that when trouble comes knocking at your door, look at it in the eye and say, **'I am stronger than you. I shall overcome you, and this too shall pass.'**

The objective of this book is to help us create an action plan to **ACHIEVE MORE**.

An action plan defines three things:

1. What you want to achieve
2. How you expect to achieve it
3. Target date to achieve it

A Win-Win Attitude

" *Winners have will power;*
losers have won't power. **"**

How is it that under the same set of circumstances some people break records, while others break themselves? The difference lies in our **ATTITUDE.**

Success does not depend on our position, but on our disposition, which is our attitude.

> *It is well said that success depends*
> *10 per cent on what happens to us and*
> *90 per cent on how we respond.*

What Makes
a Winner According to an ancient tale once, an old Indian chief was teaching his grandson, imparting wisdom about the constant battle being waged within us—between the two wolves inside each one of us. One is evil, and the other, good. The evil one is greedy,

arrogant, selfish, crooked and egoistic. The good one is peaceful, calm, happy, gracious, generous, honest and compassionate. The grandson was confused and he asked, *'Which wolf will win?'* The grandfather replied, *'Son, you have a choice. Which one wins will depend on which one you feed the most.'*

The worst kind of battles that ever take place are those within a person, those that are internal. To win these battles, we need to know who the real enemy is. Only once you strike the real enemy can you overcome your internal battles.

When you want to run away from your problems, you take a vacation; but then if you don't know how to get rid of them, you take them along with you on your vacation, carrying all that turmoil inside.

We All Have Two Natures Within Ourselves

Nature number one wants to do what is fun and convenient, which may or may not be the right thing to do and could even be self-destructive.

Nature number two guides us to do the right things that lead us to happiness, even if they are inconvenient in the short run.

But it's Nature One that predominantly takes over Nature Two. We know things that are not good and healthy for us, that mess up our lives, but we do them anyway. Our best intentions are not good enough.

In life, we need to overcome the vices that pull us down and strengthen the good that lifts us up. Many people do not understand why they don't do the good they want to do, and continue doing the wrong they don't want to. People understand and can differentiate the right from the wrong, but they still continue doing what's wrong.

Good intention with bad action is common practice. We all have the desire to be good and do good. But when we examine ourselves, we fall short. If we actually did all the good things that we already know to be 'right', then life would be a total delight.

Life would be a lot easier if the world was divided into the good and the evil. We could retain the good and get rid of the evil. But that's not the way things are. The battle inside is to do what is easy, quick and convenient rather than what is the right and the best thing to do.

> *Thinking, believing and knowing what's good is not good enough.*
> *DOING IS.*

Attitude is a Choice

A positive attitude does not mean that a person is blind to facts, nor does it mean that he has to agree with or accept everything in this world. It only means that he is a solution-focused person. It is the ability to see and smell an opportunity in every problem. It is about persistence and determination, not discouragement and depression.

Become Solution-Focused, Not Problem-Focused

Many times in life, we discover new scenery, not because the landscape has changed, but because we are seeing it from a different perspective, and the difference is in our attitude.

Attitude makes all the difference. It can make or break lives. We might understand it better by looking at the **philosophy of an ant, who sets an example of how to look at an obstacle:**

Have you ever seen an ant sitting idle? Probably not. Why? Because:

1. Ants never sit idle. It is not in their nature. They are hard working.

2. Ants never quit. If we try to block their way, they will go up, down, sideways, but they will not stop. How long do they keep trying to overcome the obstacle? Till they find a way to rise above it. So, obstacles don't stop them, and they shouldn't stop us either. They persist.

3. Ants are far-sighted. They don't think only about summer in summer. They are busy collecting food and preparing for the winter. That's why they are in a rush all through the summer season. You never see an idle ant unless it is dead.

4. Ants have a work-life balance—they work during summer and rest during winter. They hibernate to conserve energy. They know when to stop working.

5. Ants are purpose-driven—their sole job is to look for food for their mates. They don't get distracted. They are focused.

6. Ants can carry big responsibilities—although ants are small, their contributions are big. They can handle up to hundred times their body weight!

The philosophy of an ant can be concluded in one sentence—they are hardworking, purpose-driven, and far-sighted; they don't quit, and they maintain great work–life balance.

To Change Reality, You Need to Change Your Mentality

During illness we seek an exceptional doctor, during construction we seek an exceptional engineer and during war we seek an exceptional general…

What makes them exceptional? It is their attitude. Attitude is more powerful than skills, academic qualifications, good looks, place of birth, connections and everything else put together. Whenever we speak well about a man, do we refer to his looks, clothes, face or academic qualifications? No. We refer to his attitude.

Imagine that you have four glasses. The first one is plastic, the second ceramic, the third steel and the fourth silver. If you fill apple juice in each one of them, would it taste different because of the containers? The answer is no. It is not the container that decides the taste, but what is inside each one of them.

Attitude is a habitual way of thinking and feeling. **It is a viewpoint, a frame of mind, a thinking process and a way of looking at things.** It is our standpoint, our approach to things or our reaction to situations in life.

Diseases of Attitude Pessimism and negativity are as dangerous or even worse than the diseases of the body—like heart issues, blood pressure, cancer, etc. We need to learn how to handle these diseases.

Pessimistic Behaviour: Who is a pessimist? A pessimist is well defined as someone who goes to the land of milk and honey, and the only things he can see are calories and cholesterol. That's a man who is obsessed with problems and is prone to problems. There are some people in the world, who give you a problem when you present them with a solution. **They have a problem for every solution.** A pessimist says, *'It may be possible, but it's too difficult'*, whereas an optimist says, *'It may be difficult, but it's possible'*. The pessimist focuses on the difficulty, not on the possibility.

Achievers look for solutions for every problem, and losers look for a problem in every solution.

Somebody defined optimists and pessimists as brilliantly as this:

An optimist is one who wakes up in the morning, sees the bright sun shining outside and says, *'Good morning God.'* On the other hand, the pessimist is someone who wakes up in the morning, opens the window, sees the bright sun shining, and says, *'Good God! It's morning.'* They keep spreading their pessimistic attitude among others like the plague. They keep collecting and compiling tons of reasons why something cannot be done. They keep figuring out what's wrong with things. They never want to see what's right. They don't look for positives. They keep looking for negatives and are delighted when they find them. The bigger the number of negatives, the merrier they are. Why? Because they found what they were looking for. They never cherish the sunrises or the sunsets, because they are too busy seeing the spots on the window.

> *Positive people not only reinforce their attitude but also protect it from contamination.*

Why do we send our car for servicing periodically? Our car needs servicing every few months, and we need to change the oil and filter, periodically. Such preventive maintenance increases efficiency and the productive life of the car. Chances of a breakdown go down and effectiveness goes up. You optimise performance.

The big question is what's different about a human mind? Don't our minds need to be serviced periodically for rejuvenation? If not, wouldn't they burn out and break down?

Attitude goes on from one generation to the next. No wonder some families and societies are inherently positive, whereas others are inherently negative.

Stop Being Negative and Look for the Positive
There is an ancient tale about a king who had a close friend, who always looked at the positives in life. To anything that happened, he would say, '*It was for the good.*' One day, the king accidentally cut his thumb and his friend, as expected, said that there must be something good in this. The king, who was in pain, lost his temper and sent him to jail. A few months later, the king went hunting and got lost in the woods. Inside the deep forest, a tribe held him captive, to offer as a sacrifice to their gods. As the priest was tying up his hands, he noticed that the king's thumb was missing. Being superstitious, he felt that this would be an incomplete sacrifice and would attract divine rage. He set the king free. When the king came back, he introspected on his friend's remark on 'everything happening for the good' when he had lost his thumb, and felt very remorseful. He went to his friend and apologised. The king said to his friend, '*You were right. It was because I lost my thumb in that accident, that I am alive today. But wasn't it bad that I sent you to jail?*' The friend said, '*No it was for the good.*' The king wanted to know what was good about it. His friend replied, '*If you had not sent me to jail, I would have accompanied you*

on the hunting trip, and today I would have been the one to be sacrificed.'

If you analyse the story above, you will see that the objective is not to be fatalistic, but to be optimistic. Look for the positives. A positive thinker is an optimist. *We cannot always change the circumstances, nor can we change the reasons or the seasons, but we can change ourselves.*

Permanently blaming others is a colossal mistake. There are certain things that are beyond our control. If there are four seasons—summer, winter, autumn and spring—can I make them into two or ten? Definitely not! Nor can I choose my own two winters, five summers from the coming five years…doesn't work that way. We have to take things as they come.

So, what do we really need to do? We need to change our attitude and thinking. Once we change our own thinking, we stop playing the blame game. When we address the real problem, which is implanted in our own thinking, we find that life—physically, financially and spiritually—changes for the better.

W. Clement Stone, owner of a large insurance company in the US, would always say, *'That's good, what a great opportunity'*, even when something went wrong. Good, bad, right or wrong didn't matter to him. In the process, he would always consciously make efforts to look for something good and eventually find it. Somehow, his objective was to convert a bad situation into a good one, at all times.

> ## Can we always make a good choice in a bad situation?
> ## Yes, we can!

- If others want to live a petty life, then let them. But why should we?
- If others want to argue over petty things, then let them. But why should we?
- If others want to cry over petty things, then let them. But why should we?
- If others want to leave their future in the hands of others, then let them. But why should we?

Change is Uncomfortable Attitudes are patterns of thoughts or thought patterns. When we think differently, our attitude changes. But any change is uncomfortable, even a positive one. There are some people, who are so comfortable in their 'dungeons of misery' that stepping out even for freedom is uncomfortable. They suffer from 'the victim's complex', and they are permanently 'sympathy seekers'.

Those who resist a change make excuses and rebel by saying—'*I have my free will*', '*I will decide when I want to change*', '*I don't want anybody to pressurise me*' and so on.

Do We Really Live in a Free World? Are we free to choose everything in life? The answer is, absolutely not. In fact, some of the most important things in our lives are beyond our control. For instance:

- Could we have chosen where we would be born? Obviously not! But we accept it and celebrate it.
- Did our parents choose us? They probably didn't have a choice.
- We didn't choose our brothers and sisters either.
- Did we choose our neighbours? Even countries cannot choose their neighbours.
- We didn't choose the country we were born into.
- We can choose the kind of shoes we wear, but could we have chosen the time we were born?
- We can choose the colour of our car or clothes but not our skin.
- If everything were within our control, then why would an ophthalmologist wear glasses?
- Why would a gastroenterologist suffer from acidity?
- Why would cardiologists have heart attacks and cardiac surgeons go through bypass surgeries?

The only thing we have a choice in is the way we deal with the world. It is our attitude.

Bruce Lee, the great martial artist, had one leg shorter than the other by one inch, but he didn't complain. He was near-sighted and had difficulty seeing an opponent without contacts or glasses.

Despite these shortcomings, he practised 5,000 punches every day. No wonder, he became a martial arts legend. He made a choice to persist. He realised he had a problem, but he chose to turn it into a purpose.

Bruce Lee said, '*I fear not the man who has practised 10,000 kicks once, but I fear the man who has practised one kick 10,000 times.*'

> **The pedigree of a horse is judged by his breeding and training and not by a fancy stable.**

Achievers Create An Antenna To Attract Positive Thoughts And A Circuit Breaker To Disconnect Negative Thoughts.

ACTION PLAN

- Are you an optimist or pessimist?

- What three actions do you commit to that will make you a more optimistic person?

  i. _____

  ii. _____

  iii. _____

A Person With A
Positive Attitude Cannot
Be Stopped.
A Person With A
Negative Attitude Cannot
Be Helped.
In Other Words, A Person
With A Positive Attitude
Is Unstoppable

CHAPTER 2

Life is Funny
—Let's Get Started...

"The lines on our palm do not decide our
future. There are those without hands who
not only write their own futures,
but also those of others. **"**

**Put the Man
Together** One day, a young executive
came home with a bag full of
work. He had a five-year-old boy who wanted to play
with him. The executive tried to explain to him by
saying, *'Son, I've got a lot of work to do. I'm behind in
my office.'* The son replied, *'Dad, when we are behind in
school, they put us in a slower group. Why don't they put
you in a slower group?'* The father responded, *'No son,
it doesn't work that way in the corporate world.'* Unable to
understand the reason, the child insisted on playing
with his dad. The father wanted to find a way to get
rid of the kid for some time so he could catch up with

his work. He saw a magazine lying next to him with the picture of the world on top. He called his son, showed him the picture, tore it up into pieces and said, *'Son, go put this picture of the world together. When you are done, I'll come and play with you.'* He knew this couldn't be done easily, and even if it could, it would still take him many hours to complete. The kid went to put the map together and the father got busy with his work. Surprisingly, within a few minutes the kid came back and said, *'Dad, I am done.'* The father was shocked and said, *'Son I don't believe it. I've got to see it.'* When the father saw that everything was indeed all done to perfection, he said, *'Son I've got to learn from you. How did you do it?'* The kid said, *'Dad it was easy. On the other side of the picture of the world was a picture of a man. All I did was put the man together, turn it upside down and the world came together.'*

What appeared so complicated and time consuming to the father was literally 'child's play' for the son, who came up with a very simplistic solution. But the spirit of the story is different — **when people are thinking right, things fall into place and solutions start emerging.**

Life is funny. For as long as we are alive, we keep learning how to live life. Life continuously teaches and tests us in varied situations, such as the breakdown of a relationship, a serious illness or the loss of a loved one.

Is there anyone who has not been on an emotional roller coaster while experiencing all or some of the above? None!

Such experiences can either make a person become better or grow bitter. What can a person do when he faces a situation that seems like a dead end? Further, how can a person convert his setbacks into comebacks? How are a few people, unlike most others, able to convert obstacles into opportunities, and problems into possibilities? They are able to do so because they are prepared and possess 'win-ability' skills that consist of—their attitudes, resolves, resolutions and commitments among others.

Work the Idea

Once a student asked a teacher, *'How can I achieve my potential? I want to be a great writer.'* The teacher asked the boy, *'Do you know where the greatest potential lies?'* The student said, *'Yes, of course, in schools and colleges.'* The teacher said, *'That's not true. Come, I'll show you where the greatest potential in the world lies.'* He took the student to a cemetery and said, *'Look at all these people lying here; they all had great potential. They wanted to become great artists, athletes, musicians, writers, and entrepreneurs. They all lived and died with the philosophy – "I could have", "I should have", but "I didn't". They died with the potential in them.'*

An idea dies unless it is acted upon. The best idea will not work unless we work the idea.

Price for Success

There was a massive oak tree at the centre of a village. While the villagers enjoyed the shade provided by the large tree, they took its existence for granted as it had been around for decades. However, one day, unexpectedly, it came crashing down. The shocked villagers soon made some meaningful discoveries. Although the tree had seemed healthy externally, termites had rendered it hollow on the inside. The villagers understood that the tree had obviously not decayed overnight. They also realised that had they nurtured and protected the wonderful tree, they could have enjoyed the shade for a long time to come. They lost the tree because of their indifferent attitude.

> *If we are not willing to pay the price for success, then whether we like it or not, we will have to pay the price for failure. A price has to be paid, no matter what.*

We need to clearly understand that success does not only depend upon special skills, formal education or superior intelligence. If this were true, our world would not be populated by so many unsuccessful, yet highly educated and skilled people.

If we examine the life histories of successful people, we will find that they share some common qualities and behavioural patterns. Therefore, following these common qualities is one way of ensuring success. Similarly, unsuccessful people share some common behavioural traits. Therefore, we can save ourselves from failure by avoiding these traits.

Ancient wisdom says that God gave us two ends—one to think with and the other to sit on. Success depends on 'which end we use the most'.

Achievements do not come by default; they are first learnt and then practised. The miracle of being healthy and wealthy begins with learning the process that leads to success; it is ongoing till death.

A good life is not measured by bank balances and material possessions alone. It is measured by our attitude towards life. It is both a philosophy as well as an idea to live by.

Life becomes worthwhile only when we plan our lives. When we do this, we are sure to achieve incredible results. However, if we do not plan our lives, there is a strong probability that we will automatically become a part of someone else's plan. In other words: **We should live by design not by default.**

When people fail, it does not necessarily make them failures. This is because failing can often be treated as a detour, but never as a dead end. We might have failed, but that does not mean that we are failures. Therefore, **the probability of failure should not stop us from striving for the possibility of success.**

Winners are not afraid of losing, but losers are afraid of winning. Losers consciously want to win, but subconsciously they don't believe they can. Since, they don't believe they can win, they start half-heartedly and end up losing anyway. Then they justify it by saying, *'I knew I couldn't do it, but I gave it a shot'*, converting their belief into a self-fulfilling prophecy. They sabotage their own success, because they are afraid of winning.

> **Most people see opportunities, but very few seize them.**

Often, one of the most painful moments of our life is when an opportunity knocks on our door and we find ourselves unprepared. If we are not prepared when the opportunity comes and start preparing then, it's too late.

Success is achieved when opportunity is complemented with preparation. However, those who are unprepared, blame their luck. Every victory is the result of the following components—sacrifice, self-discipline, hard work, commitment, integrity and responsibility, besides our willingness to invest time, effort and money. Only when we are prepared with such qualities can we fetch abundant and gratifying returns. There are no free lunches in this world. Without preparation, one can neither consistently achieve success nor sustain it. Obstacles test our preparedness to successfully convert the obstacles into opportunities.

Michelangelo, a great Italian sculptor, achieved mastery by choosing hard work and sacrifice, and rejecting mediocrity. Had he chosen mediocrity, nobody would have remembered him. When we accept mediocrity, we become mediocre people with mediocre achievements. Most successful achievers are those who wanted to quit but did not. The greater our preparation, the greater is the probability of us achieving success in life.

Wouldn't it be a lot better if we prepared ourselves early in life? It is aptly said that youth is often wasted. By the time a person gains maturity and good sense, youth is gone. Considering this truism, youngsters can lead much more useful and fulfilling lives.

Human beings do not realise how and when they become teenagers. As teenagers, we believe that we have all the answers and solutions to the world's problems, not knowing that, most of the time, we don't even have the right questions.

In our twenties, we often do not know where we are. We are neither here nor there, or we are either here or there. In our thirties, we want to make money and raise our families, but wonder how we missed out on our twenties. In our forties, our shapely bodies change, our stomachs become wider than our chests, we grow double chins, dancing no longer holds the same degree of enticement, while music seems to be more noise than melody. In our fifties, our childhood friends become grandparents and many of us go through surgeries; however, we prefer to call them procedures! In our sixties, music still seems like loud sound. However, it no longer bothers us as we have started losing our hearing. We want to take it easy, but we do not know what is easy. In our seventies, we retire. We have breakfast at 11 o'clock, lunch at 4 o'clock and dine at 10 o'clock. We are lost! We prefer window-shopping as a pastime. We enjoy eating soft food—ice creams and yoghurts. We wonder where our kids are. In our eighties, we suffer strokes and wonder what's next. That is when we begin to realise that years have passed by much faster than days and weeks.

That's when we also realise that living a meaningless life is akin to merely existing. In fact, it is only waiting for death. In life, everyone needs to make a choice every day, between keeping busy with living or waiting to die.

Only a meaningful life gives fulfilment. Life without fulfilment is empty. It is like good looks without goodness.

Confusion Personified Unfortunately, some people who live lives of confusion expect success. However, it does not happen this way.

This is a typical example of a confused dad who wrote the following 'howlarious' letter to his son: '*Dear Steve, out of consideration, I am writing this letter slowly because I know you read slowly. I read in the newspaper that most accidents take place within 10 miles from where you live. So, we have decided to move. I don't have the new address because the previous family that lived here took the house number with them when they moved so that they wouldn't have to change their address. The jacket that you wanted me to courier to you, your aunt thought was too heavy to send with the zippers. Therefore, we cut off the zippers and put them into the jacket's pockets. Your sister-in-law just had a baby, but I don't know what it is yet. Therefore, I cannot tell you if you've become an aunt or an uncle.*'

This story might sound exaggerated, yet many people live their lives in this fashion. This story is a classic example of stupidity and ignorance in action. **To some people what appears to be clear thinking may be nothing short of clear confusion.**

> *There is something called warped or messed-up thinking.*
> *For example:*
> *Foolish people think exercise is useless.*
> *If they're well,*
> *they think they don't need it.*
> *If they're sick, they can't do it anyway.*
>
> ———
>
> *There is a strange kind of confidence that emanates only out of ignorance.*

Martin Luther King Jr, an American civil rights activist, said, '*Nothing in the world is more dangerous than sincere ignorance and conscientious stupidity.*'

It is said that 'ignorance is bliss'. Well, it's really not true. In my opinion, ignorance is misery and a disaster — go ask a lawyer, what we don't know can hurt us a lot in life. Go ask a medical doctor, what we don't know can hurt us a lot in life. Therefore, ignorance is not bliss.

In fact, there is nothing more dangerous than stupidity and ignorance in action.

No matter how hard you try, **ignorance cannot be concealed** and **wisdom gets revealed.**

People who inhabit our world can be categorised under various heads. They can be:

1. Talkers or doers
2. Leaders or followers
3. Those who leave footprints, or
4. Those who leave butt prints

Finally, there can be those who **design their lives** or those **who live their lives by default**. All of us fall into one or a combination of these categories. We need to decide which group we want to belong to.

There remain two more types of people with whom we share our planet—Success Seekers and Failure Avoiders.

1. **Success Seekers:** Success seekers are those who play to win out of inspiration. They are motivated, optimistic and hopeful. They have a burning desire; they have fire in their bellies. They are doers; they are action-oriented. They are enthusiastic and inquisitive. They have a competitive spirit and finish what they start. They keep asking themselves, 'What if?', 'What if?', 'What if?' They want to be better, faster and smarter than the best. They obsess, eat, drink and breathe their passion; no wonder they become unstoppable and end up being winners. They may or may not be good leaders, but they are **ACHIEVERS. They leave footprints, no matter what they do or where they go.**

2. **Failure Avoiders:** Failure avoiders are those who go through life playing not to lose. They play out

of desperation. They only have a preference but no conviction. They have a very casual approach to life. They give up at the slightest obstacle. They are laidback and complacent, and they are neither good leaders nor good followers.

'You miss 100 per cent of the shots you don't take,' said Wayne Gretzky, the famous Canadian professional ice-hockey player.

Next, there are three kinds of people based on the quality of success:

(a) Unsuccessful
(b) Temporarily Successful
(c) Significantly Successful

The significantly successful are the ones with substance and character. **They sustain success, leaving the world a little better than how they found it.**

This book will help us learn how to be a success seeker and not a failure avoider!

Achievers Recognise Opportunities And Seize Them.

ACTION PLAN

- Are you a success seeker or a failure avoider? Explain for the purpose of self-evaluation.

- Please take out some time and reflect on the answers to the following questions:

  i. Do you think you're leading a
     meaningful life?   YES/NO

  ii. Whatever you do, do you do it
      half-heartedly?   YES/NO

  iii. Do you have clarity of purpose?   YES/NO

- What aspects of your life are you living by default?

  i. _____

  ii. _____

  iii. _____

- List three positive lessons that you have learnt that will help you live by design.

  i. _____

  ii. _____

  iii. _____

CHAPTER 3 ———————————————————

Gist of Life

Problems are a Sign of Life Forty years ago, in Toronto, I heard Dr Norman Vincent Peale, the author of the book *Power of Positive Thinking*, speaking. I was a part of the audience. He must have been around five feet three inches tall, and maybe in his eighties at that time. His speech drastically influenced my life. His enthusiasm and conviction made me revise the definition of 'height', thereafter. I learnt that we must never measure a person's height neck-down but always neck-up. His self-confidence, clubbed with humility, taught me that confidence without humility amounts to arrogance. He said to an audience of close to a thousand people, '*You people look pretty calm and relaxed, it seems no one here has any problem.*' Then he asked, '*Does anyone here have any problem?*'

Well, who does not have problems?

Everybody raised their hands. Then he asked, '*How many of you would like to get rid of your problems?*'

Everybody raised their hands again. He stated, '*On my way here to this congregation, I came across a place where people were lying in peace, totally relaxed and stretched out. They had no problems, whatsoever. How many people would like to know where this place is?*' Everybody raised their hands again. To everyone's surprise he said, '*Two blocks away from here, there is a cemetery where people are lying stretched out, totally relaxed and without problems.*' He asked, '*How many people would like to get rid of their problems now?*' Nobody raised their hands. What he said thereafter was insightful: '*Problems are a sign of life. So long as we are alive, we shall have problems. The day we have no problems, we will be dead.*'

When we are running short of problems, it is time to watch out. That's the time to get on your knees and ask God, '*Don't you trust me anymore? Why don't you send me some problems?*'

Dr Peale continued, '*We cannot solve all our problems, but we certainly can handle them.*' That day he gave out a prayer by Reinhold Niebuhr called the *Serenity Prayer*, which is probably hundred years old, and which to me, literally, is the essence of life.

> *God grant me the serenity to accept the things that I cannot change, courage to change the things that I can and wisdom to know the difference.*

I have been using this prayer since the day I heard it and it has been a source of great strength to me. If we analyse this little prayer, we will discover that it contains the **Gist of Life to Live By**. Let's analyse it line by line.

The first part of the prayer, *'God grant me the serenity to accept the things I cannot change'*: There are some things in life that we just cannot change. They are beyond our control and are called fate. For example, I didn't choose my parents. I also didn't decide where I was going to be born. I neither chose the colour of my skin, nor my height. I didn't choose my gender, my date of birth or my date of death. That's the way things are. Sometimes people are born with a physical deformity. Sometimes bad things do happen to good people for no fault of their own. What wrong did they do? Who knows? **We cannot choose the cards that are dealt to us; we can only choose how to play the game**. Just like how we cannot choose the direction of the wind, but we can always choose how to set the sail. Sometimes life gives us a lemon; the choice is ours to either cry or make a lemonade!

Keep in mind that we need to strike a balance between what we need to accept and what we can change. Often, we keep fighting the things that we just cannot change or that are beyond our control, and by not accepting them graciously, we bring stress into our lives. If we cannot change them, then we should accept them graciously, not grudgingly. Here, the appropriate behaviour is acceptance and surrender. Surrender does not mean we are defeated. It only means we have accepted graciously. We also have the opposite choice of not accepting and getting upset.

If we miss our flight, we have a choice to get mad, shout and be frustrated, or just accept it graciously. Either way, the reality remains the same regardless of whether we accept it or not. This outcome was neither desirable nor intentional. Count it as a blessing then.

Helen Keller was once asked, '*How come you made such contributions to the world in spite of being blind, deaf and mute?*' She communicated, '*It was not in spite of, but because of.*' In other words, had she not been blind, deaf and mute, she probably might not have made such contributions to the world.

The second part of the prayer, '[**Give me the**] *Courage to change the things that I can*': If I can change it, then why brood about it? Give me the courage and guts to change it.

And the last part of the prayer, ' *... wisdom to know the difference*': There should not be any confusion between what I can change and what I cannot. It is wisdom that helps us make the right choices and makes life livable.

Two thousand years ago, Roman philosopher Cicero had said that everything in life falls into two categories:

1. **Things we can do something about and**
2. **Things we can do nothing about**

If we analyse Cicero's philosophy, we will figure out that if we can do something about it, then — why worry? And if we can do nothing about it, then — why worry? It is beyond us.

What Franklin Roosevelt said just adds to the essence of Cicero's philosophy, *'Men are not prisoners of fate, but only prisoners of their own minds.'*

Often, our external circumstances are the result of our thought process. It does not mean that we are a hundred per cent in control of our circumstances. Our life is both a result of **Fate** and **Free Will**.

1. **Fate is the cards that are dealt to us (not our choice)**
2. **Free will is the way we play the game (our choice)**

Is there a science behind being happy and successful? The answer is yes. If we accept graciously what cannot be changed, and change courageously what can be, we would be happily successful.

Life is Full of Choices and Full of Compromises Life is full of choices and full of compromises; although it seems like a contradiction, it really is not. Even a compromise is a choice. **Every choice we make and every decision we take, there is a trade-off and a pay-off.**

1. If I treat you badly I've chosen to be treated badly.
2. If I over eat, I have chosen to be obese.
3. If I smoke, I have chosen to invite cancer.
4. If I lie, I have chosen to fall in my own eyes.
5. If I drink and drive, I have chosen to invite an accident.
6. If I treat others with disrespect, I have chosen to be treated with disrespect.

7. If I have a casual attitude, I have chosen to invite casualty.

8. If I am careless, I have chosen to become negligent.

Whereas,

9. If I exercise, I have chosen to strengthen my body.

10. If I have positive thoughts, I have chosen to be mentally strong.

11. If I am careful, I have chosen to take pride in performance.

12. If I am honest, I have chosen to be trustworthy.

13. If I eat healthy food, I have chosen to invite good health.

We could go on and on...

Olympic champions could have wasted their time watching TV, attending parties, taking drugs and alcohol. But they chose to make positive choices and, hence, they won the gold. **A series of positive choices result in success and a series of negative choices result in failure. Success or failure is an effect of choice**.

> *We are free till we make choices.*
> *After that, the choice controls us and*
> *we have no more choice.*

All through life, every day, we make hundreds of choices. The kind of work we do, the kind of friends we have, the places we live in, the food we eat, how much we eat, the clothes we wear, the time we go to bed and whether we exercise or not. They are all choices.

Once we choose not to study for the exam and we fail, we need to be ready to bear the consequences of the wrong choice. When we habitually start making negative choices, we start rationalising and making excuses.

The choices we make by default are as important as the choices we make by design. Why? We still have to bear the consequences, no matter what.

Achievers Are Willing To Accept Short-Term Pain For Long-Term Gain.

ACTION PLAN

- Write three positive choices that if you practise daily will propel you towards achieving more:

  i. _____

  ii. _____

  iii. _____

- How will the above choices make you feel?

  i. _____

  ii. _____

  iii. _____

CHAPTER 4

The Wisdom Truth

" *The mind, once expanded to the dimensions of larger ideas, never returns to its original size.* **"**
— *Oliver Wendell Holmes*

If we keep doing what we have been doing all our lives, we will keep getting the same results that we have been getting. If we want different results in life, we need to either **do different things or do things differently**.

When we get unwell, the doctor prescribes us medicines and a diet. Not just that, he also asks us to do everything differently. For example:

1. We've been eating all our lives, but now we need to eat differently.
2. We've been walking all our lives, but now we need to walk differently.
3. We've been taking decisions all our lives, but now we need to take decisions differently.

4. We've been thinking all our lives, but now we need to think differently.
5. We've been breathing since we were born, but now we need to breathe differently.

Now, since birth, we have been thinking all right, but going forward, we need to think, talk, walk, eat and work differently. The desire to conform is evidently present in most of us, but in reality, utmost progress has been stimulated by non-conformers. Anything different reflects originality and innovation, but not all different things have merit or are good.

> *All progress is change,*
> *but not all change is progress.*

Education is what makes us do things differently. The objective of education is to bring transformation, not just awareness. When we are exposed to any information for the first time, it brings awareness. Awareness is knowledge — knowledge of 'now I know'. When we internalise the information to bring about a behavioural change, it results in transformation. Till then it is only information. **Knowledge is information, understanding is comprehension, and wisdom is putting them into action.**

Chanting or Cheating? There was a young priest who kept chanting the holy scriptures with folded hands, day in and day out, believing that he was acquiring holiness. One day, the head priest sat next to him and started rubbing two stones against each other. The head priest did the same thing continuously for days. Ultimately, the young priest could take it no more and worriedly asked the head priest, *'Why are you doing this?'* The head priest said, *'I am trying to make a mirror out of this stone.'* The young priest said, *'But that's not possible. It can't happen. How can you make a mirror out of stones?'* The head priest replied, *'Son, you are absolutely right. Just the way I cannot make a mirror out of these stones, remember, you shall not become a holy person by just mechanically chanting scriptures. You will need to put your learning into practice.'*

Our learning must result in positive actions. **Unless one's behaviour changes, learning has not taken place. Knowledge without action is like ploughing without sowing.**

Spirituality There is a fascinating story of a supposed spiritual teacher who saw a diligent woodcutter in a forest. He thought to himself, *'What a great opportunity to indulge in some spiritual teachings.'* As the woodcutter kept painstakingly chopping the wood and piling the logs in his wagon, the teacher kept preaching the gospels. As the woodcutter was packing up after work, the teacher asked, *'Have the sermons converted you into a spiritual person now?'* The woodcutter said, *'Since morning, all you've done is talk endlessly about spirituality, but not once did you think of extending a helping hand to* *me. I feel it's you who is in dire need of learning about spirituality and its facets.'*

The difference between a spiritually evolved person and someone who is not is easily visible. Spiritually evolved people internalise their concepts of truth that result in their behaviour and actions. They do not put on a false mask to pretend to be spiritual. The true meaning of spirituality is a combination of **three core values — integrity, responsibility and respect.**

Principled people do not have to proclaim to the world their spiritual conduct. The world makes its own judgement. A lighthouse does not call for attention, it just radiates, and the world takes notice. Likewise, spirituality is self-evident in one's behaviour.

How can one have a growth track without a spiritual track?

Anything done well with integrity, and that which adds value to life, is spiritual. For example:

- A politician who thinks of the next generation rather than the next election is practising spirituality.
- A person who makes shoes that are value for money is practising spirituality.
- A doctor who saves lives is practising spirituality.
- A judge who gives judgements based on 'what is right', rather than 'who is right', is practising spirituality.
- A husband and a wife who are honest with each other are practising spirituality.
- A teacher building the character of a student is also practising spirituality.

- A politician who puts the national interest above his own is practising spirituality.

Have You Ever Seen a Sermon Walking? In 1953, a large group of dignitaries gathered to welcome Nobel Peace Prize winner Dr Albert Schweitzer at the railway station. He was well built and six feet four inches tall. The crowd was waiting with bouquets of flowers. As Dr Schweitzer looked over their heads, he saw an elderly woman struggling with two large bags. He politely excused himself from the crowd, walked briskly, grabbed the bags and escorted the lady to the bus leaving all dignitaries behind. He returned and apologised to the dignitaries for having kept them waiting. A reporter remarked at that time, *'This is the first time I have seen a "sermon walking".'* What a message! That's spirituality.

Dr Schweitzer said, *'In everyone's life, at some time, our inner fire dies out. We should be thankful for those who rekindle the inner spirit.'*

Keeping ethical commitments is practising spirituality. When we add value to whatever we do, and that becomes the philosophy we live by, we go beyond just making money to practising spirituality.

Consequences of Compromising on Spirituality

1. You become untrustworthy.
2. You lose credibility.

3. You lose self-respect and the respect of others.

4. Your self-esteem goes down.

> ***Making money is stealing; earning
> money is practising spirituality.***

Today's world of political confusion, terrorism, family
disintegration, youth disillusionment, corporate
distrust and religious corruption have led to global
uncertainty and unrest. People choose shortcuts and
dishonest methods to make money. In our present
environment, most people want to make money, and
very few want to earn it. Just when you are in a hurry
to make money, you skip the steps to climb up faster.
Making money by hook or by crook amounts to
deviating from spirituality. Those who have gained
big bank balances out of greed and crooked means
are the ones always afraid of losing it. In my opinion,
they are not spiritual because they are always uneasy
and restless. Why? Because they have only made
money, not earned it. Peace and happiness are the
two outcomes of spirituality.

- As per the Gallup Survey, '63 per cent of people
  who go to work are "not engaged", which means
  they don't do their jobs. An additional 24 per cent
  are "actively disengaged", which means that they
  make sure that others also don't do their jobs. That
  leaves only 13 per cent of people who go to work
  and actually do work.'[1]

---

[1] *http://news.gallup.com/poll/165269/worldwide-employees-
engaged-work.aspx*

It has literally become an epidemic to see employees spending three to four hours a day checking personal e-mails and social media while they are at work. Is that what they are getting paid for? When someone steals our wallet from our pocket, what do we call that person? A thief! When we do all this, what are we?

When people do not have the right values, what do they do?

1. They lie to their employees and employers.
2. They lie to their customers and colleagues.
3. They lie to their spouses and children.

When they come to work, they take pens and pencils, supplies, staplers and stationary home; they make personal calls during company time. They go to restaurants for personal outings and bill it to the company. They fudge time sheets. Is that what they are getting paid for?

We need to understand that **wages without work amounts to stealing. Stealing is making money, not earning it.**

Making money is crooked, and earning money is spiritual.

> *Spirituality is not a strategy, it is a WAY OF LIFE.*

Achievers Practise Spirituality As A Way Of Life.

ACTION PLAN

- Identify three areas where you can integrate spirituality as a way of life:

  i. Area 1. _____

  Commit to do _____

  ii. Area 2. _____

  Commit to do _____

  iii. Area 3. _____

  Commit to do _____

CHAPTER 5 ——————————————————

Mind Your Mind

What is Mind? The Mind is like energy—it remains a mystery, is the least understood and is the most wasted. The mind is the element that empowers a person to think, feel, reason, understand and make judgements. It is intangible and abstract but it is for real.

Our mind is a thought factory generating either positive or negative thoughts. We can condition our thought factory to become either like a thermometer or a thermostat. A thermometer only reads the external temperature—it has no power to influence or change anything beyond that; it is totally helpless. Whereas, a thermostat has both the ability to read and regulate. It controls its environment.

How should our minds be—like a thermometer or a thermostat?

This is How a Thermometer Mind Works A man wakes up in the morning, sees the bright sunshine and feels happy and elated. But the next day, he wakes up and sees the weather damp and gloomy and feels depressed.

Who is controlling his mind? The external weather. He is helpless.

This is How a Thermostat Mind Works A man wakes up in the morning, sees the bright sunshine and feels happy and elated. But, the next day he wakes up, sees the weather damp and gloomy, yet feels happy and elated. Why? Because he has programmed his 'thermostat mind' to be happy and elated. So no matter what the external weather is, the weather in his mind is in his control. He is in charge of his life.

If we want to have a meaningful life, we should model ourselves on a thermostat and not a thermometer.

Go on Autopilot Many years ago, I was travelling to the US with my younger daughter who was then five years old. The pilot was known to me, and being a friendly guy, he invited my daughter to show her the cockpit. Then he explained a few things, *'When the aircraft takes off there are many unknowns, such as the clouds, the wind, lightning and thunder, and due to these turbulences, most of the time, it goes off course.'* My little daughter asked curiously, *'What happens to the* *aircraft when it goes off course?'* Then he said, *'We have something called the autopilot. Every time the aircraft goes off track, the autopilot brings it back on track.'*

Autopilot means that all positive behaviour must become a reflex action. The one, who is in charge of his life, puts his mind on autopilot. Thermostat also works as an autopilot.

Power of The Mind   The following is a positive example of the **Power of the Mind**. Many a times, during our seminars, I have had defence personnel go through our programmes. They tell me that up in the Himalayan mountain ranges, in the sub-zero temperatures they have seen monks who are able to meditate without clothes. I often wonder how they don't fall sick in such extreme conditions.

• After a series of studies conducted with the help of the Dalai Lama in the late 1970s and early 1980s, it was found that 'many Tibetan monks were able to raise their skin temperature by as much as 8.3°C, whilst keeping their core temperature the same. Other studies have shown that they can actually increase their core temperature as well. This is primarily attributed to a particular meditation technique called *Tummo*, which involves visualising the human body as a hollow structure of light, and then using a combination of breathing control methods to slow the heart rate. This is so effective that monks have actually been documented sleeping on a rocky ledge at over 4,500 metres above sea level, apart from each other with no additional insulation beyond their robes. Allegedly, they didn't even shiver, and we're talking about temperatures in the region of –17°C.'[1]

The power of the mind has always been a fascinating subject, and today it is more so than ever. The scientific community has realised the importance of the sum-total of our behaviour, health and interpersonal relationships. Thoughts, do in fact, modify and have a direct consequence on behaviour. Cultivating and practising good and positive thoughts have a direct positive impact on behaviour, environment and achievements. In fact, the managements of most companies today are convinced that in order to compete and be profitable they need to restructure and re-engineer the minds of individuals. If a man's mind is intelligently cultivated, it shall 'reap what it sows', that is, if a man thinks right, his mind will develop right thoughts and his actions are going to be right as well.

Just as a gardener sows a seed, likewise we take a thought and sow it in the field of our mind. When we plant a seed in the soil of our mind, it grows. Now, whether it becomes a mango tree, a mulberry bush, a poison ivy or a rose shrub depends on whatever we plant. If we sow a rose, it is natural that we will reap a rose. One thought placed in the mind acts as a seed for another thought. The impressions left behind by

---

[1] *http://www.keepmewarm.com/2016/06/how-tibetan-monks-deal-with-extreme.html*

these thoughts will be stored somewhere in the field of our mind, consciously or subconsciously, directly or indirectly. Depending on how this seed is watered, these thoughts will generate other thoughts, thereon.

There is a multiplier effect—**one seed does not give one fruit; the harvest is manifold, whether positive or negative**. That is Nature's Law.

Positive People Recover Faster In an article on *Healing with Positive Thinking*, Dr Ravinder Mamtani in New York, who has been leading the research in this field, says, '*In many cases if you have a chronic disease or illness, calming the mind will calm the disease or illness.*' Calming the mind means getting rid of the negative thinking, being optimistic and focusing on the positive aspects. Do that and you will heal yourself. All you have to do is learn how to be calm. Control and direct your mind so that you have a positive belief system and remain optimistic and you really do change your life. Dr Mamtani went on to find that patients who had or who developed a positive attitude and positive feelings had better outcomes and were more likely to rebound from medical setbacks.[2]

Discover the Power of the Mind Our mind has the power to make heaven out of hell and hell out of heaven. A house

---

[2] *http://www.affirmationsforpositivethinking.com/Healing-with-Positive-Thinking.htm*

becomes a home only when it can shelter the body, the mind and the soul completely.

Just like the soil does not choose the seeds that are planted, our subconscious mind does not decide what thoughts to choose. Just like a farmer decides on the seeds, the conscious mind chooses the thoughts to implant in the subconscious mind. There is a gamut of conscious choices like what books to read, what music to listen to, what friends to keep, and what movies to watch. Once we have decided what movie to watch, the conscious mind closes and the subconscious mind opens to receive. When a gruesome scene appears, we feel repulsed. Upon seeing an exciting scene, we get excited and a sad scene makes us cry. Do you think there is a magic button installed somewhere? Obviously not! The explanation is very clear—the conscious mind decides, the subconscious receives, and the body reflects. The body is a slave to the mind. It literally obeys the mind.

Our mind is like a floating iceberg of which only one-seventh is visible to the eye, and the rest is all under water. Similarly, our conscious mind is only one-seventh, and the balance real power lies with the invisible subconscious mind.

It is also essential to clean our mind. **Just like a dentist gives us a dental floss to clean our teeth, we need a 'mental floss' to clean our minds of the excessive scum it accumulates.** Mental pain and agony are worse than physical pain; so it is important to defuse the pain.

Follow the 2D approach to cleanse the mind:

1. **Develop a delete button for your negative memory:** Reflect, but do not dwell on past mistakes — develop a selective memory to accumulate successes in life, which will motivate you further, and delete the negatives and mistakes of the past from your selective memory that pull you down.

2. **Direct knowledge into wisdom:** To be knowledgeable, we need to feed our mind with something positive every day, but to be wise, we need to delete something negative from our mind every day. The process of accumulation of positives and the deletion of negatives is where the transformation from knowledge to wisdom takes place.

A farmer, even after he plants good seeds, needs to constantly de-weed his garden, otherwise the weeds destroy his good harvest. Similarly, the cleansing process of our mind should be constant and consistent.

A pure mind and evil thoughts are not compatible. Therefore, **only a pure mind will produce pure thoughts resulting in pure actions.**

Achievers Put Their Mind On Autopilot And Make All Positive Behaviour Into Reflex Action.

ACTION PLAN

- Think of three situations where you have lost control over yourself. How could you use your autopilot button to bring yourself back on track?

  i. Situation _____

    Change _____

  ii. Situation _____

    Change _____

  iii. Situation _____

    Change _____

- Commit to yourself to reflect daily.
- Commit to yourself to feed your mind daily with positive reading/listening for at least 5–30 minutes.

CHAPTER 6

Invest In Yourself

**"*If you do not like the output in your life,
then you must evaluate the input.
If you do mediocre things, you will live a
mediocre life. If you do excellent things,
you will live an excellent life.*"**

> *Every thought is a seed — if you plant
> an inferior seed, you cannot expect a
> superior fruit.*

We buy expensive clothes, designer jeans and fashionable shoes without a second thought; probably even spend thousands of dollars a year on them. We go to expensive restaurants and sometimes wait for hours to be seated. We spend a few thousand bucks and probably do so twice or thrice a week. What do we have to show the next day? Nothing, but an upset stomach and a few extra pounds.

If we invested a fraction of the money above neck that we so willingly spend below neck, we would be in a **totally different bracket**.

Input Determines Output

Where we will be five years from now will depend on three things:

1. **The books we read**
2. **The movies and shows we watch**
3. **The company we keep**

Where we are today is also the result of these three things because they represent input that leads to the output called **ATTITUDE**. Which books to read, which movies to watch and which friends to keep are the choices we make.

Don't Allow Others to Dump Trash

Suppose, one day when we are cooking in our kitchen, our neighbour walks in, dumps his garbage into our food and dirties our kitchen. In such a situation what would we do? The answer is quite obvious: We would try to stop him, we would not even hesitate to pick a fight, or we might even call the police to throw him out.

If under no circumstances would we allow anyone to pollute our food and kitchen, then why do we allow the media to pollute our minds with evil and negative thoughts? We would never like to associate ourselves with or allow in our homes those who have negative minds but they literally come into our homes through television and other media to poison our minds.

> **Do not make your mind a dumping ground for someone else's trash.**

Many times, the so-called liberal minds argue that the garbage being shown on media does not have to be watched or listened to when you have the option to switch it off. They say we have choices and can watch what we want. The question is, do we really have choices? To what extent do we have choices? Or, is it only a justification to continue polluting? This is like saying, '*I will pollute the air, but if you don't like it, too bad – you can stop breathing. I am living in a free society. I have the choice to do what I like with my life.*'

In the real world, it does not work that way. We are all connected in some form or the other. What I do affects you and what you do affects me. When we cut forests in one part of the world, it changes the climate of another part. A disrupted balance could change the equation between life and death.

Is It Only My Life?

Let us assume we are travelling on the high seas in a boat with ten people. Far out into the sea, one person pulls out a drill and starts drilling a hole under his seat. Obviously, with everyone's life in danger, we ask, '*What are you doing?*' He says, '*I am only drilling under my seat, which I paid for and not under yours, and I have the right to do what I like under my seat. It's my life.'* What a joke! His selfishness has gone to the point of blinding him to reality and making him stupid enough to eventually self-destruct. He doesn't realise that the consequence of his behaviour could be fatal and he himself could drown alongside others.

Answers of this nature have become epidemic in every area. Isn't this totally irresponsible and selfish behaviour? Individualism has superseded the larger interest. **The 'me and mine' has superseded the greater responsibility.** How can society not be affected by what is happening all around?

Our Mind is a Thought Factory

Obscenity in – Obscenity out
Garbage in – Garbage out
Good in – Good Out

Unfortunately, 'garbage in and garbage out' is not always true. Often, 'garbage in, garbage stays and garbage grows', and it breeds within us. This multiplier effect is dangerous and destructive. Our mind is a thought factory. Whatever we input into the factory decides the output. The input being books we read, shows we watch and friends we keep, and the output being our attitude.

The Books We Read

According to a research, on an average, a self-made millionaire reads two to three books a month, which comes to approximately twenty-five to thirty books a year. In thirty years, that comes close to a 1,000 books. They just don't read any book. They read self-help books that help them grow in life. We all know how to read, but very few actually do read, and of those who read, very few know what to read.

> **A good book shares the wisdom of the ages in a capsule form.**

How to Read a Book and Get the Best Out of it

1. I have a principle in my life—I never lend my books to anyone nor do I borrow any. The reason is that whenever I read a book, I always underline, mark and make notes on the side. When someone offers to lend me a book, I thank them, but then politely request them to give it to me, gift it to me or sell it to me because I tell them I will not return it and if it is not acceptable to them, then I refuse to accept the book. My books are my treasure, I refuse to share them.

2. I always sit down with a highlighter in hand while reading a good book. I always underline, mark and make notes on the side. Why? Because some day when I will refer to it again, I will not have the time to go through the entire book again and will only look at the underlined portions and notes. Besides, searching for the important material, in case it's not been underlined or highlighted, is a waste of time anyway. By making notes and underlining, you only reinforce your take-home.

3. Another thing I've learnt about reading a book is that if the first chapter really does not entice me, or I feel I've not received much value from the first chapter, I stop reading it. At one point of time, I used to continue in the anticipation that maybe I will find something in the next chapter ... or the next chapter. But it does not happen that way. A book is generally ten to fifteen chapters long of maybe 150–200 pages. The first chapter would be about one-tenth of the book. If I do not receive any value out of that, then I will probably not get much value out of the entire book. It's not worth my time.

4. Additionally, in order to focus and concentrate, and insulate yourself from other distractions, switch off your mobile. Distractions dilute your power to absorb. They are the biggest danger towards achieving more. A major differentiating factor between winners and those who are not is the ability to concentrate and focus. What the winner achieves in one minute with concentration cannot be achieved in four minutes by unfocused people.

Look at the Power of Concentration and Focus

On a bright sunny day, when we hold a magnifying glass over a piece of paper and keep hovering it over the paper, nothing happens. But the moment we hold it steady, the rays of the sun get focused and the paper immediately catches fire.

The Shows We Watch

Look at some of the rock music and rock bands — can we even repeat the lyrics of many of those music groups or are they too obscene to be recited? Yet, we allow either ourselves or our kids to watch and listen to the obscenity being fed through the media. No wonder, our kids and we ourselves behave so obscenely and crudely these days.

But the big question is on the subjectivity of obscenity — how obscene is obscene? A little obscenity is OK, but too much is not? Obscenity is obscenity. Acceptance of it on any level is totally wrong.

A study shows that almost 90 per cent of rapists are addicted to pornography. Pornography has become an epidemic and is a big business. Because of the big money involved, there is a lot of vested interest in the sex industry. A few people argue in favour of pornography and claim that pornography and art are the same. Is pornography subjective? Someone asked a judge, '*Can you define the line between pornography and art?*' And the judge replied, '*I cannot define the line, but I can easily tell the difference when I see the two and yes, there is a lot of difference.*' Pornography objectifies and degrades women, while art uplifts them.

Addiction to pornography is a progressive disease like drugs. The only message that pornography has is that 'a woman is an object of sex to be used, abused and discarded'. Pornography changes the meaning of sex from being sacred to perverted.

Look at Soaps: What are soaps? Soaps are nothing else but bed hopping from one person to another. If you have any definition of morality then you find that soaps are only glamourising immoral behaviour. If you have no definition of morality, then it is a different issue. If we keep watching this kind of immoral behaviour day in and day out, they become our benchmarks. No wonder, we start behaving that way. Premarital sex, extramarital sex and divorces have gone up as an impact of these soaps.

- In the article, *'Soap operas and their effect in our society'*, it is said, 'Successful soaps tend to be smartly written, sexy and replete with plot twists and love triangles, including domestic violence against women generally speaking. In the best-case scenario, the show becomes popular, and viewers begin to incorporate some of the themes into their lives.'[1]

Soaps have led to the breakdown of the family unit and made our society more crime and drug prone. They are all the results of evil thoughts that are implanted into our minds through a negative environment.

Toxic input is damaging to our output. We need to stay away from toxic thoughts and people. We need to flood our minds with enriching and positive material.

---

[1] *https://challenges.openideo.com/challenge/womens-safety/research/soap-operas-and-their-effect-in-our-society*

> *We have to insulate our minds from*
> *negativity by being careful of*
> *the things we watch.*

The Company We Keep

It is well said that **bad company corrupts character**.

Winners surround themselves with winners who live their lives based on values and have the ability to influence their destiny. If every weekend, we spend time with our friends moaning, groaning and complaining about how bad our jobs, bosses and our lives are — is it going to inspire us?

When we leave, do we feel that we are going away motivated? If the answer is no, then it is time we do away with such company. Negative influences are so subtle that one does not even realise that each time we interact, we get pushed further into the wrong direction with a wrong attitude.

Change is Subtle Just imagine what would happen if we throw a live frog in a bucket of boiling hot water? The frog will jump out because of shock. But if we put a live frog in a bucket of water at room temperature, and then start heating it from below, the temperature change will be so gradual that the frog will not even feel it, and will eventually die in the hot water.

Many of us may or may not realise that we have friends who are nice, well-intentioned people but

have negative influences on us. By the time we realise
that we have been eroded from within, it may be too
late. We need to make choices early in life about the
kind of friends we want to have. Every relationship
has either a positive or a negative influence on us.
We need to surround ourselves with people much
wiser than us or join a group of people who have high
performance standards. Remember, a good friend's
attributes start rubbing off on you. They relax you
and their company is food for the soul. Both stress
and calmness are contagious. If we are always around
stressful people, our own stress levels will go up. We
need to stay away from negative, selfish, dishonest
and insincere people, because their influences start
impacting our character. **Avoid people and situations
that bring conflict.**

**Input
Governs
Output**
An eagle's egg was placed in the
nest of a prairie chicken. The egg
hatched and the little eagle grew up
thinking it was a prairie chicken. The
eagle did what the prairie chickens did. It scratched
the dirt for seeds. It cried and cackled. It never
flew more than a few feet, because that is what the
prairie chickens did. One day he saw an eagle flying
gracefully and majestically in the open sky. He asked
the prairie chickens, '*What is that beautiful bird?*' The
chickens replied, '*That is an eagle. He is an outstanding
bird, but you cannot fly like him because you are just a
prairie chicken.*' So the eagle never gave it a second
thought, believing it to be the truth. He lived and

died as a prairie chicken, never knowing what he was capable of. What a waste! **He was born to fly high but conditioned to crawl on the ground.** The same thing is true for most people. If you want to soar like an eagle, you have to learn the ways of an eagle. The prairie eagle was born to win, but conditioned to lose[2].

Some people are like owls. They go blind in sunshine. They cannot see the daylight. They are born with an inability to see anything positive.

Every day when we wake up, we choose the weather in our minds — whether we want to have a good day or a bad day. There are people whom we ask, *'How are you today?'* Their answer is either *'Under the circumstances'* or *'Under the weather'.* The question is, what are you doing under there? Some would respond, *'Well, based on the weather report, it's going to be a bad day. It's going to be too hot or too cold or too muggy.'* For such people, the weather bureau decides their life every day, because they do not exercise their choice to have a good day. Such answers depict helplessness.

Are our thoughts building us up or tearing us down? Wrong thoughts will bring misery. A man who is miserable only makes those around him miserable. Those who become victims of such misery are generally family members, business associates and society at large. Negativity keeps filling our mind with evil and destructive thoughts. **We need to have a circuit breaker that disconnects the negative thoughts.** A circuit breaker disrupts the connectivity

---

[2] *You Can Win* by Shiv Khera.

when there is a short circuit to prevent damage and resumes functioning again once the problem is fixed.

Our life has a lot to do with our attitude, which results in our actions and, hence, the consequences. Our actions cannot be left to the mere idea of chance or luck; they should rather be designed by thought.

> *More important than the harvest we reap are the seeds that we sow every day.*

Be Vigilant In Choosing Your Thoughts And Judicious In Choosing Your Inputs. A Healthy Mind Has The Capacity To Significantly Achieve More.

ACTION PLAN

- The books we read, the shows we watch and the company we keep will define where we will be in five years.

  List down three books, three shows and three people that have uplifted your life.

  i. Books

  _____

  ii. Shows

  _____

  iii. Company

  _____

- Make a list of three of your closest friends and ask the following questions. After you have the answers, think about how each one has impacted your life.

  i. Are they intrinsically positive or negative?
  ii. Are they overtly critical?
  iii. Are they egoistic?
  iv. Are they balanced?
  v. Do they pull your spirits down or lift you up?
  vi. Are they living their lives based on principles of integrity?

  1st person _____

  2nd person _____

  3rd person _____

  Going forward, would you like to keep them in your life?

You Have To Be A
Winner Internally
Before You Can Be
One Externally

CHAPTER 7

Making of a Winner

Winners Make Things Happen, Losers Wait for Things to Happen

Vince Lombardi, the famous American football coach, once said, *'Winning is not a sometime thing; it's an all the time thing. You don't win once in a while; you don't do things right once in a while; you do them right all of the time. Winning is a habit. Unfortunately, so is losing. Some guys play with their heads but you've got to play with your heart. Running a football team is no different than running any kind of organisation – an army, a political party or a business. The principles are the same. The object is to win fairly and squarely by the rules – but to win. I firmly believe that any man's finest hour is that moment when he has worked his heart out in a good cause and lies exhausted on the field of battle – victorious.'*

> *When something bad happens,*
> *it can break you,*
> *define you or strengthen you.*

Who said winning came easy to those who won? Every person has the potential to find his true capacity. **Yes, we were born to win, but to be a winner you need to strive and strike with a positive attitude.**

What Makes a Winner?

1. High Self-Esteem

What is self-esteem? Self-esteem is a feeling of self-worth. Just like air, high self-esteem is essential for survival. It empowers a person and reflects every action. It is the foundation stone of our psyche on which our behaviour rests. It is acceptance of our intrinsic value.

Self-esteem is the way we feel about ourselves. When we feel good, the world looks nice, productivity goes up, and relationships are a lot better. And the reverse is just as true.

The foundation of self-esteem lies in self-acceptance. What does that mean? It means that 'I accept myself the way I am.' Self-acceptance doesn't mean complacence or arrogance. Self-acceptance does not mean 'That's the way I am' and 'That's the way I will be'. 'If you don't like it, too bad, take it or leave it' amounts to arrogance. Properly understood and analysed, self-esteem is the epitome of humility.

It is based on the following principles:

1. I have no idea how I came into this world — it's a mystery, but I am here and I'm here to stay.

2. By no standard am I perfect.

3. **I made mistakes. I make mistakes. I'm not proud of my mistakes. I learnt from my mistakes. I will not repeat my mistakes. I apologise and seek forgiveness for my mistakes. But I am not a mistake.**

None of us is perfect. There are certain things we are born with such as our height, skin colour, shapes of our faces and so on. They may not be ideal. Some of them are beyond our control, which means we didn't create them, nor can we change them. May be we can try to improve on them to an extent but we cannot do away with them. In such a case, we can either keep fighting what we cannot change and bring turmoil or accept them as our identity and build on them.

The lack of acceptance creates an identity crisis. Identity crisis is the beginning of all problems. The moment we practise self-acceptance, we overcome our internal turmoil and are at peace with ourselves. We feel complete and adequate. We don't have to prove anything to anyone in the world. Again, this is not arrogance, because we are willing to learn and improve. Because of self-acceptance, we have our own identity. We're not looking for validation from outside, which means we are internally driven.

We Need To Become Internally Driven, Not Externally Driven

We should get our validation from inside, not outside. What does that mean? One day, if someone gets up in a great mood, calls me and says, *'What a great job you're doing and I feel proud to call you a friend.'*

How does it make me feel? I feel wonderful.

But supposing the next day, the same person gets up in a bad mood, calls me up and says, *'You rascal, you cheat, you crook. You are the biggest fraud in town.'*

How does that make me feel? I feel terrible.

So, who's controlling my life? Obviously, the other person, because when he calls me up and gives me a compliment, I feel great. But the next day when he calls me a crook, I feel rotten. That person is in control of my life. Is this the way I want to live? Obviously not! Now don't get me wrong. When he says, *'You're the greatest guy'*, it is nice to hear those words; but if he doesn't, I still feel good. Why? Because in my own eyes, I'm a good human being. On the next day, when he rips me apart, he is not able to because in my own estimation, I'm still a good human being. **I'm getting my validation from inside, not outside. I'm internally driven not externally.**

Self-Acceptance Gives Identity

Charlie Chaplin, one of the world's greatest comedians, was passing through a European country where he saw an advertisement for a Charlie Chaplin look-alike competition. Out of sheer inquisitiveness, he decided to participate. There were close to 500 people participating. To his total surprise, he came at number 7. Charlie Chaplin wrote in one of his memoirs that when he came at number 7, he was taken aback. He wrote, *'We live in a world where showmen succeed and a real man fails. For a moment, even I got confused if I was the real Charlie Chaplin or the six before me. Then I realised that though the other six could copy my looks and moves, none of them could match my mind and my attitude.'* Charlie's attitude was driven by high self-esteem, which came from self-acceptance and gave him his identity.

He wrote, *'I could laugh at life. I loved losing more than the winners enjoyed winning, because I knew I was the real Charlie Chaplin.'*

One can even love to lose when one knows what one's real identity is. Charlie Chaplin didn't feel threatened as he didn't have to prove anything to anyone. He writes further, *'More than my appearance, my mind and my attitude give me my identity.'*

He was not looking at acceptance and validation from the world outside; he knew who he was. He knew his identity, so it didn't matter to him who won. People who live with self-acceptance have high self-esteem — they are stable and balanced. They are at peace with themselves.

2. Consistency

How do you define winning or failing?

The recipe of becoming a winner or a failure is

simple, but not simplistic. Simple means that 'it's easy to understand and implement', whereas simplistic means 'underplaying the importance of it'.

Recipe for Success

The Recipe is –

A few positive actions repeated daily result in winning, and a few mistakes repeated every day result in failure. Notice two important keywords here — **'repeated'** and **'daily'** — repetition is the mother of learning. We should recognise the extraordinary power of repetition. Repetition brings consistency and consistency results in proficiency; it is proficiency that really shapes our lives.

Winning and failing are not **events** but **processes**. They are **journeys** and not **destinations**. They don't happen overnight.

Nobody becomes successful by doing something positive once in a while. Look at most multinationals — they started modest and gradually by constantly practising discipline became global giants. If we look at the martial arts student's journey, from a white belt to a black belt, we learn that it is the outcome of consistent practise for years.

It's Self-Discipline and Consistency Similarly, nobody becomes a failure by doing something wrong once in a while. Consistently repeating an error has its own compounding effects.

For example, we hear all the time, 'An apple a day keeps the doctor away.' If that is true, then what's the problem? But what's easy to do, is also easy to neglect. It obviously doesn't say, 'A candy bar or an ice cream a day keeps the doctor away.' So we cannot fall for the candy bar a day and we should not. Moreover, if we switch the two and make an error of judgement by having a candy bar instead of an apple, we will be inviting trouble. When we make an error for the first time and nothing unfortunate happens, we justify it by saying, *'Look nothing happened to me.'* But just because it didn't happen one day, does not mean that the statement 'An apple a day keeps the doctor away' does not hold true. Imagine repeating the error of having a candy bar instead of an apple daily. What do you think would be the consequence? You'd keep on adding calories, maybe become obese, and invite illness.

We also hear all the time, 'Exercising thirty minutes a day keeps the doctor away.' Again, it is easy to do, but it is also easy to neglect. It doesn't say watching TV for half-an-hour a day keeps the doctor away. If we don't exercise for one day we justify it by saying, *'I am in good health, nothing has happened to me.'* Just because something didn't happen that day, does not mean the statement 'Exercising thirty minutes a day keeps the doctor away' is not correct. And if we continue this same error, can you imagine the compounding ill-effects? The consequential health and financial cost all put together is going to be gigantic.

Bear the Consequences No Matter What!

A jellyfish sometimes swallows a snail. The snail, because of its tough shell, stays protected and alive inside the jellyfish. To sustain itself, the snail starts eating the jellyfish from inside consistently and daily, and keeps growing till a day comes when it consumes the entire jellyfish and the fish is no more. **Just the way the jellyfish destroys itself by swallowing the snail, a negative attitude eats us from within until we self-destruct.** The question is — did the jellyfish choose its own destruction consciously? Probably not. But that's immaterial. It still had to bear the consequence no matter what. Isn't the same principle applicable to our lives too? The destruction of the jellyfish is not an event but a consistent process.

Repeated errors of judgement lead to cumulative disasters. It doesn't matter whether the errors pertain to health, finances, or relationships — the damage will be evident.

It is our attitude that reflects in every sphere of life and that decides the end result. People, who are callous or careless with their health are most likely to be callous in other areas of their lives too. People who are callous about their relationships experience broken bonds. People who are careless with their finances suffer losses. Hence, a good attitude can take us places and a bad one can pull us down.

> *We need to distinguish between what's good and what's pleasant.*

Interestingly, we find that most people know the difference between good or bad, right or wrong. For example, everyone knows that exercising regularly is good for health, but how many do it? Not many. But then, why don't they do it? Because exercising every day takes discipline, which is not pleasant.

We make choices between:

- The gym and the couch
- Saving and spending money
- Eating a carrot and a cake

Life is often a choice between the good and the bad, the right and the wrong, the spiritual and the evil.

> *A series of positive choices is called success, and a series of negative choices is called failure.*

- If I don't eat an apple a day for thirty days and then eat thirty apples in one day, is it the same thing? Or can I even eat thirty apples in one day? Obviously not!
- If I don't exercise for six months, I cannot do six months' worth of exercise in one day. If I abuse my body for ten years, can I recuperate in ten days? Is it even possible to reverse the ill-effects? No, never!

We also realise that having a piece of chocolate cake every day could add hundreds of calories, and may not be good for health, but we still have it. Why? Because it is pleasant, we enjoy it. Interestingly, however, after we have it, remorse creeps in. **We need to understand that everything good may not be pleasant and everything pleasant may not be good**.

Recipes for Disaster

In one of my leadership programmes, there were close to a hundred people. I asked, '*How many believe that exercising every day is important for our health, please raise your right hand.*' All hands went up. Then I asked, '*Since everybody knows what the right thing to do is, how many exercise every day, please raise your left hand.*'

Guess what, how many hands went up? Only ten.

It raises a question—people know what to do and what's in their best interest and yet they don't do it. What is the missing component? *It's self-discipline and consistency.*

If we exercise every day, which we should and we could, we invite good health, but if we don't or if we won't, we invite disaster. If we don't, it means we are careless or we have a bad attitude. If we won't, it means we are thick-skinned and arrogant. At the end of a few years, we'll find out that our carelessness and negligence towards our health has led to an accumulative build-up of disasters. Overlooking or ignoring what ought to be done is an intentional wrong we commit at our end.

'Could do' and 'should do', but 'don't do' and 'won't do' are the recipes for disasters. So the bottom line is to achieve success, where instilling discipline is the key—we need to start eliminating the errors and inculcating discipline within. Our attitude will decide whether we go a long distance or fall in a pit.

From the above examples, it is very clear that there are some dos and don'ts in life. All these behavioural patterns are not subjective—they are universal. They have a cumulative effect.

A wise man once said, '*For every one wrong done or a mistake made, we need twelve corrective actions to counter or neutralise it. Sometimes, even twelve corrective actions are not able to counter it.*' Can you calculate the cumulative effects? The power of compounding is astronomical.

3. Self-Control

Self-Control is the Essence of Self-Respect

There is an ancient Indian story to illustrate self-control. Once an obnoxious man abused a saintly person rather harshly. The saint was very calm and relaxed. After the man finished abusing him, a passer-by asked the saintly man, '*This man abused you so harshly, how did you maintain your cool?*' The saintly man replied, '*If you give a gift to someone and they refuse to accept it, then who does the gift belong to?*' The passer-by said, '*The giver.*' The saintly man said calmly, '*I refused to accept his gift.*' The abuser realised that the abuse he directed towards the saintly man was actually self-abuse. What a real life demonstration of self-control by the saint!

> *Doing something permanently damaging while you're temporarily upset is foolish.*

Let us look at another example of self-control. Once a teacher asked a young boy, *'Who is the most powerful person in the world?'* The boy had watched a lot of TV and proudly said, *'Batman.'* The teacher said, *'Well, not really. Try once more.'* The boy said, *'Spiderman.'* Again the teacher said, *'Not really, try again.'* The kid thought this time he just couldn't go wrong, and said, *'Superman.'* The teacher said, *'Son, give it one last try.'* The boy gave up and asked the teacher, *'Why don't you tell me who the most powerful person is?'* The teacher said, *'Son, the most powerful person in the world is the one who has control over his thoughts and emotions.'* In other words, one who has self-control has the ultimate power.

To achieve balance and stability, one needs to exercise self-control in every area of one's life. It cannot be achieved overnight, but one can move towards the objective one step at a time.

Self-control at a moment of anger could prevent a life time of regret and sorrow.

> *Self-control is mastery and calmness is power. The less external masters you have, the more in control you will be and the more peaceful you shall be.*

4. Self-Discipline

One of the most critical ingredients for winning is self-discipline. **The biggest advantage of discipline is not what it 'can' do for us, but what it 'will' do to us**. It is not what we get, but what we become. A primary cause of failure is lack of discipline. Discipline is the foundation upon which the entire structure of winning is built.

There are only two kinds of pain in life. One is the pain of discipline and the other is the pain of regret. Guess which of these is more painful? Well...obviously, the pain of regret. The universal truth is that — **discipline is the remedy for regret**.

> *Self-discipline and self-control are a WINNING combination.*

No One Achieved Anything without Self-Discipline

Manny Pacquiao, one of the world's greatest professional boxers of all time, is the only eight-division world champion in the history of boxing, having won eleven major world titles. Just before going into one of his championship fights, he had said, *'I believe I can win.' 'Faith is my motivation to win.'* What do you think was the reason of his unwavering faith? His faith in winning was backed by strict action and constant training. He said, *'If you practise hard, you can win every battle.'* You think he could have become a champion without practising discipline in diet and training? Never. It's constant effort put into practising discipline over years that make you win battles. Pacquiao had once said, '*Life is meant to be a challenge, because challenges are what make you grow.*' If there is life, there will be challenges. He said, '*Only in death will I relinquish my belts.*'

We only become proficient when we overcome challenges. Just the way we practise discipline to better our skills to overcome challenges, the champion boxer polished his mental and physical skills by making discipline an integral part of his daily life.

Discipline Gives Freedom

There is a misconception that discipline takes away freedom. In fact, the reverse is true. It actually gives freedom. If I took a nice big box of chocolates for my three or four-year-old child who loves chocolates, chances are that he would like to have the whole box in one go, considering that he is a child. If I let my child have the whole box at one go what will happen? He will fall sick; but if we discipline the child to have two or three pieces every day, he will enjoy it a lot longer and maintain good health too. Did discipline take away or give freedom? The answer is quite obvious. It gave freedom.

Aristotle, an ancient Greek philosopher, said in simple words, '*Through discipline comes freedom.*'

> **Desire without discipline is only wishful thinking.**

- Can a musician be a good musician without self-discipline?

- Can an athlete be a good athlete without self-discipline?

- Can a doctor be a good doctor without self-discipline?

The answers are quite obvious. Reading through the life histories of successful people, we find that they had tremendous self-discipline to do what needed to be done, whether they liked it or not. The dictionary defines self-discipline as the 'ability we have to control and motivate ourselves, to stay on track and do what is right'. The reason why most people fail to accomplish what they want to accomplish is because of lack of self-discipline. Self-discipline is not easy, but it helps us achieve our goals by overcoming temptations along the way.

5. Passion

What is passion? Passion is a strong emotion—emotion is an energy, which propels us to commit to ourselves. If we need to achieve anything or get somewhere in life, we need to clearly have a focal point and go after it with all we've got. Whatever we do, we must put our hearts into it. If we put our hearts into it, only then it will open new opportunities. People say, *'If I had a better job, I would put my heart into it.'* It is an illusion. That's why **people do a half day's job and collect a full day's salary**. No wonder, they do not get anywhere in life. Trying to motivate people who lack passion is like resurrecting someone from the dead. It's like putting in all your energy to inflate a balloon with a hole in it; no matter how much sweat you put in to blow it up, it will not go up. *You inflate, they deflate, you inflate they deflate!*

Winners Don't Do Different Things, They Do Things Differently

Many years ago, the world record for high jump was 7 feet 4 inches. Not pole vault, but high jump. The question is, how can a human being clear a bar 7 feet 4 inches high? Even 4 feet 7 inches is tough. Someone asked the champion, *'How do you clear a bar 7 feet 4 inches high?'* He replied, *'I throw my heart over the bar and my body follows.'* What an answer! Is there any coincidence that he was a champion? In fact, with passion in his heart, how could he not be a champion?

What is the Difference between a Labourer, a Craftsman and an Artist?

According to St. Francis of Assisi, *'A man who only works with his hands is a labourer. A man who works with his hands and his head is a craftsman; but a man who works with his hands, his head as well as his heart, is an artist.'* If we want to do anything well in life, we have to work with the passion of an artist.

The Making of an Achiever

Internal struggle is an ugly battle we fight within ourselves, because it is the result of our personal imbalance. It is the condition we need to overcome. We need to have the courage to identify and overcome the causes that create such struggles. Once we realise that the cause of struggle is not external but internal, we realise that it can be eliminated one step at a time. Keep in mind that the struggle is a response that is learnt, consciously or subconsciously, over a period of time. It is a programmed attitude.

We All Think Of Changing The World, But Achievers Consistently Work On Changing Themselves.

ACTION PLAN

- Write down three things you commit to do to enhance your self-esteem.

    i. _____

    ii. _____

    iii. _____

- Write down three areas where you need to practise self-control to achieve more.

    i. _____

    ii. _____

    iii. _____

- Write down three areas where you need to be more consistent in order to achieve more.

    i. _____

    ii. _____

    iii. _____

- Can you think of three areas in your life that would improve drastically if you exercised self-discipline?

    i. _____

    ii. _____

    iii. _____

- What do you feel passionate about? Are you pursuing your passions?

Keep It Up

**❝ *Achievers achieve,*
no matter what. ❞**

The road to victory is not easy. It is strewn with obstacles and pitfalls. Winners condition their minds to do the right thing, consistently.

The problem is not the lack of awareness to distinguish between right and wrong, but the lack of putting **'what is right'** into action.

Conditioning the Mind A teacher called two students who were both looking for direction in life. One was a bully and the other, docile. The teacher gave appropriate directions to both. The docile student understood, accepted, obeyed and implemented it respecting the teacher's guidance. The bully told the teacher, *'I have no confusion in understanding what is right and wrong. I know what's right, but I'm not attracted to it. On the other* *hand, I know what's wrong, but I'm attracted to that. My biggest problem is that I don't feel like doing what's right, and somehow, I cannot prevent myself from doing wrong. My problem is very different.'*

Why is the bully having this problem?

What is the moral of the story?

The moral of the story is very clear — **conditioning the mind is more important than will power**. Hence, we need to be conditioned to do the right thing.

Examples of Negative Conditioning:

- A doctor who smokes is knowledgeable and understands the implications, yet he smokes.
- A policeman who drinks and drives is knowledgeable and understands the implications, yet he drinks and drives.
- An athlete who abuses drugs is knowledgeable and understands the implications, yet he takes drugs.

> *People with clear purpose and goals succeed because they know the destination and they have clear direction.*

Overcoming Weaknesses No human is perfectly positive nor perfectly negative. We have a little bit of both within us. Through their thought process, winners overcome their limitations and focus on their strengths, whereas losers recognise their strengths but focus on their limitations. By not correcting one major weakness that holds us back, we would probably neutralise all our strengths.

What's holding us back?

Eleven Mistakes That Hold Us Back in Life

1. **You cannot build yourself by crushing others:** If you build yourself by crushing others, you will be ripped apart, bit by bit. This is short-sighted, and you will self-destruct. The only way to become the tallest building in town is to create a strong foundation, and build the tallest structure, or to crush and destroy all others, and by default, become the tallest building in town. But if you crush others, they will not let you survive or thrive. They will come and rip you apart. Trying to pull others down instead of lifting yourself up is both unprincipled and self-destructive.

2. **Worrying about things that cannot be changed:** Worrying equals to two unproductive days — today and tomorrow. Many of the worries are imaginary. They only create illusions of a problem.

3. **Just because we are unable to do something, we think it is impossible:** We create imaginary barriers justifying the task as impossible. Our inability to do a certain thing does not mean that it is not doable. Anyone who ever told you that **'you cannot'** said it because **'he could not'**.

4. **Majoring in minor issues:** We waste life unnecessarily by majoring in minor issues. We need to rise above petty and trivial matters.

5. **Neglecting self-development:** Just the way our bodies need food every day, our minds need positive thoughts every day. Neglecting self-development or personal-development leads to degeneration and degradation.

6. **Forcing others to believe and live as we do:** Thrusting, penalising and coercing others to live by your beliefs shows closed-mindedness and arrogance. It also demonstrates oppressive behaviour which emanates from insecurity.

7. **Taking false credit:** Not acknowledging the efforts of others and taking undue credit for their work is selfish and lacks integrity.

8. **Avoiding and ignoring your duties:** Doing 'what is pleasurable to do' and not 'what ought to be done' is reckless behaviour. It shows a lack of integrity and amounts to irresponsible behaviour.

9. **Favouritism:** Being blind to fairness is detrimental to growth. Favouritism reflects on you as a person — it shows either bias or vested interest.

10. **Passing the buck:** Not willing to accept responsibility, blaming others and hiding behind excuses is a typical behaviour of irresponsible people.

11. **Encroachment:** Disregarding other people's space and dignity, bulldozing and grabbing forcefully what is not yours is larceny.

These are only eleven shortlisted mistakes among many more. The objective of identifying these mistakes is to reflect and learn from them, and eventually eliminate them. Who said wisdom comes with age?

Wisdom comes only from reflecting on and learning from our past mistakes. Some people only grow older with age and not wiser.

Wise people challenge themselves to grow and achieve more.

Challenge Yourself to Greater Heights

It is said that Professor Abraham Maslow used to challenge his students by asking questions like these:

1. Which of you is going to write the next book?
2. Who is going to be like Dr Albert Schweitzer?

Listening to these questions, the students would either giggle or blush. That's when Dr Maslow would clarify expectations by telling them what he meant. He would ask, *'If not you, who will?'*

Shouldn't we ask the following questions to ourselves?

- If not us, then who?
- If not now, then when?
- If not here, then where?

> *Achievement lies in practising excellence in the smallest details.*

We Need to Distinguish between LITTLE and CRUCIAL, as against PETTY and TRIVIAL

Little and Crucial I know a billionaire who owns many properties. As he was walking through his factory premises, he saw some scrap papers on the floor. He stopped to pick them up. He didn't call anyone to instruct them to pick up the papers. He just did it himself. Analyse his behaviour. What message did all his staff get? **Small details do matter**. They saw leadership by example. It inspired everyone to pay attention to the smallest details.

Remember, **little things are not little**.

- **An army of the best soldiers with arms cannot fight and win the battle if they have no shoes.**
- **It is the small leak that sinks the ship.**
- **It is the small spark of fire that destroys the forest.**

Have you ever been bitten by an elephant? Probably not. Have you ever been bitten by a mosquito? The answer is that all of us have been, and many times. It is the little, little things that make the big difference. If they make such a big difference, how can they be little? What a paradox!

Don't **major in minor things** does not mean ignoring the little that is important but means distinguishing between **little and crucial** and **petty and trivial**.

Once, one of the computers at our office didn't have a functional UPS (uninterrupted power supply) and we asked the concerned person to fix it. But instead of rectifying the problem, he plugged the computer directly without bothering to fix the UPS. He shrugged off the responsibility by saying, *'It's not a big issue. It's just a little thing.'* The question is, when does it become a big issue? When the computer blows up because of a voltage fluctuation or when we lose important data? Do accidents inform you in advance before they happen? And if an accident does happen, just imagine the loss.

Is that what we're waiting for? How short-sighted and irresponsible! What a callous attitude!

A few questions arise here:
- If the loss happens, who is accountable for it?
- Who compensates for the financial and productivity loss?
- Would just an apology in a callous situation like this be acceptable?

That person in the office looked at the issue as **'petty and trivial'** and not **'little and crucial'**.

These situations evidently happen in many offices — ignoring small, little things that are crucial is sheer negligence and can be disastrous.

It is much easier to do the right thing the first time, every time, than to explain why we did not and repent later. People of integrity live by the philosophy — PREPARE AND PREVENT RATHER THAN REPAIR AND REPENT.

Petty and Trivial

Some people major in minor issues. We need to learn what to look for and what to overlook. We let insignificant things bother us to the point of becoming unmanageable. We respond with frustration, anger or outrage, because we become emotionally disturbed. This is because we become reactive, not proactive. Sometime, you also find people behaving irresponsibly. A common example is that people set appointments, but neither do they show up on time nor do they have the courtesy to call. Often, little, unpleasant surprises happen. Do not let them throw you off track.

Don't try to kill butterflies with guns. The dogs bark, but the caravan goes on. We must not let every petty issue bother us. Keep little things in perspective. We cannot let little inconveniences such as minor delays, setbacks and disruptions bother us.

Little glitches will always happen in life. If you give them more importance than they deserve, they will only heighten your stress and shorten your life. They will only increase irritability and decrease stability. One must always make allowances for them and avoid stress.

When we learn to distinguish between a problem and an inconvenience, we learn to distinguish between little and crucial, and petty and trivial.

Overcome Self-imposed Limitations

Self-imposed limitations bind us down. It is not unusual to see that most records are set by people who are ignorant about their limitations. **When we put a limitation on what we can do, we put a limitation on what we will do**. There are many examples present in nature to validate this thought. According to scientists, the bumblebee's body is too heavy and its wingspan too small for it to fly. Scientifically, the bumblebee just cannot fly, but the bumblebee doesn't know that, and it keeps flying anyway.

When we don't know our limitations, we go out and achieve something, and then wonder if we actually had a limitation to begin with. Well, there are a few people who are born with disabilities that may limit them in certain ways, but even then they choose to rise beyond their limitations and create history by achieving new heights. It is easier said than done but it is doable. Stevie Wonder was born blind, but that didn't stop him from becoming one of the most famous singers of our time. The only limitations a person has are those that are self-imposed. Self-imposed limitations are connected to self-esteem—the lower you value yourself, the lower are the expectations you set for yourself.

Self-imposed limitations could result from many factors like flawed education, the people we hang around with, and so on. Mental limitation is also a big blinder to future breakthroughs; believing in ourselves and setting high standards will help us break past self-imposed limitations.

The greatest achievers probably faced much bigger problems than what most of us faced or would ever face in life.

- Steve Jobs, creator of Apple, was a college dropout, and yet created history.
- Bill Gates, co-founder of Microsoft, was a college dropout too, and yet created history.
- Albert Einstein, theoretical physicist, was dyslexic, and yet he created history.
- Leonardo da Vinci, the celebrated painter, was dyslexic too, and yet he created history.
- Michael Phelps, an American champion swimmer, fractured his wrist prior to the Olympics, and yet created history. He said, *'If you dream as big as you can dream, anything is possible.'*

The Difference Between The Good And The Great Is The Attention Given To Details.

ACTION PLAN

- On a scale of 1–10, rate yourself and analyse your personality. Anything below '5' is poor, and would imply that it requires a lot of improvement.

  i. Do you help those who are less fortunate than you are? `1 2 3 4 5 6 7 8 9 10`

  ii. How often do you ignore your duties? `1 2 3 4 5 6 7 8 9 10`

  iii. Do you play favourites? `1 2 3 4 5 6 7 8 9 10`

  iv. Do you give credit where it is due? `1 2 3 4 5 6 7 8 9 10`

  v. How often do you let obstacles derail you? `1 2 3 4 5 6 7 8 9 10`

  vi. Do you finish what you start? `1 2 3 4 5 6 7 8 9 10`

  vii. Do you let petty issues bother you? `1 2 3 4 5 6 7 8 9 10`

  viii. Are you a constant worrier? `1 2 3 4 5 6 7 8 9 10`

  ix. Do you focus on self-development? `1 2 3 4 5 6 7 8 9 10`

  x. Do you encroach on others? `1 2 3 4 5 6 7 8 9 10`

- Based on the above analysis, make three action commitments that you will practise for the next thirty-one days.

  i. _____

  ii. _____

  iii. _____

Be Open To Change But Stay Firm On Values

CHAPTER 9

Valuations Change, Values Don't

" *Majority opinion does not make the right wrong or the wrong right.* **"**

A young accountant was once offered a large sum of easy money for a job that made him somewhat uneasy. It wasn't quite illegal, but the contract struck him as questionable. So he requested the client to give him a day to decide. That night, he went home and told his mother about the terms and conditions of the contract and the big money that was involved. His mother was totally illiterate. After listening to him for two hours she said, *'Son, I don't understand anything of what you just said. The final decision is yours. All I can say is one thing — that every morning when I come into your room, I find you fast asleep. I have a very hard time waking you up. I would hate to come into your room one day and see you awake. You decide.'* With these words, the mother left the room. After the mother left, the accountant kept thinking about what his mother had said. A few minutes later, he walked up to his mother and said, '*Mom, I got my answer.*'

Values are intrinsic to our lives. They add strength to our character. Values are principles that guide our actions. Positive values result in positive behaviour leading to positive consequences. They build a positive society. Negative traits such as cheating, dishonesty and selfishness result in negative behaviour leading to negative consequences. They build a negative society.

Valuables Come and Go, Values Don't

Valuations of all material properties such as stocks, bonds, real estate, commodities etc., keep changing. Some of them even change by the hour. Through generations, some values have been crystallised, which pave the way to clearly show us our dos and don'ts. Whenever we talk of values, we refer to **Universal** and **Eternal** values, which don't change with time or calendar.

Universal means that 'they cut across country, culture, and religion'.

Eternal means that 'they were here before we came, and they will be here after we're gone'. There are no new truths. Sometimes, we need to be reminded of the old ones.

Once I was being interviewed, and the interviewer asked, '*Are you saying there are some rights and wrongs?*'

I said, 'Yes. *There are some grey areas, yet there are some very clear areas. There are rights and wrongs.*' He said, '*Haven't you heard that statement by Shakespeare where he says, "There is nothing right or wrong, your thinking makes it so?" You're contradicting Shakespeare. How do you explain yourself?*' I said, '*I just disagree with Shakespeare. If there are no rights and wrongs, then every criminal in this world ought to be released. Who said they are wrong? You say they are wrong, they didn't think so — go keep arguing for the rest of your life. If there were no rights or wrongs, then Hitler was totally right. Who says he was wrong? You think he was wrong, he didn't think so. Go keep arguing for the rest of your life. Let me share with you an example closer to home — supposing you leave this studio and somebody on the street sticks a knife into your body and twists it three times. With blood oozing out of your body, you tell him, "My friend you're doing wrong." And he says, "Haven't you read Shakespeare? Nothing is right or wrong, your thinking makes it so." Try explaining it to him now. Someone creates a few widows and a few orphans and you tell him, "My friend you're doing wrong." And he says, "Nothing is right or wrong, your thinking makes it so." Go tell it to this person.*'

Benchmarks In science, we look for theories and laws. In the commercial world, we look for quality, standards, and benchmarks. Why then should we not look for universal benchmarks for values? Whatever business or profession we may be in, unless we have clear quality standards and benchmarks, how can we ever achieve them? Similarly, unless we have universal benchmarks for values and ethics, how can we ever meet them? The question is how do we set those **universal benchmarks**? I heard the following story, which clarifies the point:

There was a frail, elderly lady with two bags of groceries in her hand, waiting for a bus. Right behind her was a big boy also waiting for the bus. The bus came and they both got in. It was totally packed, but there was one seat available at the far end, so the elderly lady started moving to get that seat. The big boy came from behind, threw his big arm around the lady, took one big step, and then another, and took that seat. The elderly lady fell on the ground, her bag of groceries got scattered and she was lying on the floor totally helpless. There were many passengers in the bus. One of them was a sophisticated lady who started thinking, *'How clumsy of this boy!'* She was looking at the etiquette and the manners of the boy. There was a lawyer in the bus, who started thinking, *'There must be a law against this kind of behaviour.'* He was thinking from a legal perspective. There was a surgeon in the bus, who started thinking, *'This lady must have broken three ribs.'* He was looking from a surgical perspective. The fourth person in the bus was a psychiatrist, who started thinking, *'This boy is psychotic and he needs mental help.'* He was looking from a mental perspective. Four people thinking in four different ways—etiquette, legal, surgical and mental.

Not one of them asked this question—was this behaviour right or wrong? Why don't we ask this question? The moment we do, we become judgemental. If our value system is clear, what is wrong in being judgemental?

Two questions arise from the story above:

One: Should this boy have behaved like this with the lady? The answer is a no.

Two: Should anyone behave like this with anybody at all? The answer is a no.

If the answer to both questions is a definite no—we have found our universal benchmarks. The same principle applies to all areas of our life. Where is the confusion? Clarifying values is not tough, what is tough is to face up to them, and that's why we choose not to clarify.

Are you aware that every doctor who graduates anywhere in the world has to take the 'Hippocratic Oath' or the 'Oath of Hippocrates', which was given almost two thousand years ago? How long is that oath? Just about a page. If we read that oath, do we need any more values than that?

Every lawyer takes the oath of code of conduct all over the world. How long is that oath? Just about a page. If we read that oath, do we need any more values than that?

Subjective Values

People who have subjective values claim that it is wrong to be judgemental. They say, *'Who am I to decide?'* *'Who am I to judge?'* *'Aren't there always two sides to everything?'* All the above excuses smell of indifference, not neutrality. When somebody asks us a question, *what is the downside of lying, stealing and cheating,* what do we say to that? Do we say:

1. Let's do a cost benefit analysis.
2. Whatever works for us the best?
3. Whatever makes us feel good?

Absolutely not! But if we do and if these are the values that we live by, how do we expect the coming generation to learn any better? That means one has to come out of the shell of indifference, and not just say or do what one feels good about.

> *'If you are neutral in situations of injustice, you have chosen the side of the oppressor. If an elephant has its foot on the tail of a mouse, and you say that you are neutral, the mouse will not appreciate your neutrality.'*
> *— Desmond Tutu*

On issues of values, if a person stays neutral, it is cowardice. Even though there are some grey areas, yet there are some very clear areas too. To identify the clear areas, we must establish some benchmarks.

Just as truth does not change with the seasons, facts do not disappear just because they are ignored. The same holds true for good values. Unlike success, which is fleeting, values endure. Today's concept of relative values says, 'Everything is OK. What's right for me may not be right for you.' If values are subjective and they keep changing from person to person and situation to situation, then it means we have no values at all.

Universal and Eternal Values are Not Subjective

Peter Kreeft, a professor at Boston College, in his book *Making Choices* writes that '...contrary to popular belief, there are some clear values'. Once, just to prove his point, he made a statement in his class, '*All women in my class flunk.*' Immediately everyone protested, '*Not fair!*' So, he asked them, '*Who defines fairness?*' The class was left confused.

If fairness is subjective then there can be no universal values. The students, in this case, would have no right to impose their opinion on their teacher and neither would the teacher have the right to impose it on the students. But if universal objective values called justice and fairness exist, then the teacher would certainly be held wrong. In the absence of universal objective values, all that the students could do was protest against the teacher's rule, because their subjective standards were different from his. In this example, the question was not of liking or not liking the rule, but of fairness. The objective values remain steady eternally irrespective of personal intent. They hold true for everyone, alike. What makes acts like murder, rape, torture and oppression crimes? The fact that they fail the universal benchmark of universal objective values — fairness and justice.

> ## *Downgraded values cannot be remedied by money.*

In today's time, people are willing to bypass values in the interest of expedience and short-term gains. Hence, they are willing to act against their values. It seems that many CEOs, for example, are under such intense pressure to deliver short-term gains that they are easily willing to compromise on values.

Ray Kroc, the founder of McDonald's franchises, set a great example of values.

It is said that once Ray Kroc visited one of his franchises and found a dead fly on the floor. Soon after this, he cancelled the franchise.[1]

The way I see this is that Kroc said in unsaid words, *'All over the world people walk into McDonald's because they trust its good quality and hygienic food. If the owner of this franchise does not believe in these values, he does not deserve to carry a McDonald's name.'* In other words, what he was saying, *'Let me take my name off and see how many people go into this restaurant then.'*

---

[1] *https://ffbsccn.wordpress.com/2010/06/20/ray-kroc-and-the-parable-of-the-dead-fly-a-lesson-too-late-for-bp%E2%80%99s-tony-hayward-to-now-learn/*

> *If you ever want to lend anything to anyone in life, lend your money, but never your name. Why? Because, money is easy to recover, but name is very hard to recover.*

The message drawn from the above example is clear that there is no compromise on quality and values. You talk of flexibility, there is none. Ray earned credibility and was trusted, because he stood firm on values. Unfortunately, today too many people lack what Ray Kroc had. VALUES.

Values Are More Important Than Valuables.

ACTION PLAN

- Identify three values that you want to live by:

  i. _____

  ii. _____

  iii. _____

- Think of three incidents where you have compromised on your values. Going forward, how would you handle similar situations differently?

  i. _____

  ii. _____

  iii. _____

- Make three commitments that will put your values into actions.

  i. _____

  ii. _____

  iii. _____

Choose Character

Once a teacher asked a student, *'How does a country get destroyed?'* The student said, *'When an enemy from outside throws a bomb at it.'* The teacher said, *'No, try one more time.'* The student said, *'When an enemy from outside fires a missile at it.'* The teacher said, *'No son, try one more time.'* The student said, *'I give up.'* The teacher said, *'The bombs and the missiles are violent ways of destruction, but here is an easier way of destroying a country. All one needs is to make dishonesty a way of life, and legalise corruption and cheating. When we allow our students to cheat, they come out corrupt.'*

That is when the following examples become a reality:

1. In the hands of corrupt doctors, a sick person becomes a target, not a patient.
2. In the hands of corrupt engineers, buildings collapse.
3. In the hands of corrupt judges, injustice is done.
4. In the hands of corrupt scholars, religion is sold.

5. In the hands of corrupt police officers, criminals flourish.
6. In the hands of corrupt politicians, nations perish.

The biggest enemy of character building is a corrupt education system — **when national character is corrupt, the nation self-destructs**.

There's an old saying: '**When wealth is lost, nothing is lost. When health is lost, something is lost. When character is lost, everything is lost.**'

> *Strength of character is the foundation of all great achievements.*

Building Character   Character is not a gift, it is an accomplishment. It is built bit by bit through hard work. Once a lady took her five-year-old son to the principal of the school for admission. She asked the principal, *'When is a good time to start teaching character building to my son?'* The principal asked, *'How old is your son?'* She said, *'Five years.'* The principal said, *'Lady, you are five years too late.'*

People of character live by ethical and moral values. They rely on their internal value system to differentiate between the right and the wrong. Their clarity of values reflects in their decision making in all aspects of their life.

Character builds self-respect, which, in turn, leads to high self-esteem. Character is a composite of qualities such as integrity, honesty, ethics, conscience, loyalty, mental strength, grit, courage and many more.

> *Character is easier kept than regained.*

It is like trust — once broken, it is very hard to rebuild.

It is like credibility — once you lose it, it is very hard to restore it.

One may be able to restore credibility and trust, but character once lost is gone forever.

Character — Nature Or Nurture?

Character is not something we are born with, it is a 'learnt' behaviour. Character is based on our value system. Our values come to our aid when we face the real world.

Life is a moral and spiritual journey. A complete training of the head and the heart is needed to build a sound character. It does not make sense to hope that we will stumble onto something that will eventually generate lasting values. A good and strong character is the result of practising good behaviour with discipline.

When we find ourselves on unfamiliar grounds, it is our character that helps us identify our own and other people's strengths and weaknesses. It provides us the wisdom to identify what's good for us. It teaches us what to look for and what to overlook, when to fight and when to walk away, when to take advice and when to make our own decisions.

Myth — **W**e often hear that 'adversity builds
Adversity character'. This statement has very
Builds little truth in it. Adversity reveals more
Character character than it builds. An athlete does not prepare at the time of competition. He only reveals his preparation at the time of competition. He keeps on practising and preparing all his life and builds a reserve. When he competes, he utilises his reserve and displays his preparation.

Character is not built at the time of adversity. It is like a reserve that is built throughout one's life. When there is an adversity, we can overcome the adversity if we have built a reserve of character. If not, then the adversity will overpower us. A general does not prepare at the time of war, rather preparation starts a long time before the war is even declared. Preparation takes place during peace time.

Character helps us overcome the temptation to go off-track. Character can be well described as 'what a person would do or not do even if they knew they would not get caught'.

Character development does not happen overnight. It takes time and effort. It is not easy, but the rewards are priceless. In any good society, enduring values can only be sustained through effective character education. **The three pillars of character are — integrity, respect and responsibility.** These are the core values. Core values are principles to live by;

they are the foundation from which all behaviour emanates, resulting in consequences. Examples:

Integrity: A person of integrity will be honest and sincere. He will always tell the truth. He will walk his talk. He is genuine. The consequence of this will be that he will be trustworthy and will gain credibility. This equation applies to everything in life.

Respect: A person who lives by the principle of respect, respects himself, respects others, respects the environment, etc. Empathy is a behaviour that emanates from respect. The consequence of this will be that he will be a good human being, a pleasing personality and an asset to society. He will be easy to live with and shall have better relationships.

Responsibility: A person who lives by the principle of responsibility keeps his commitment. He becomes reliable and dependable. The consequence of this will be that you can count on him and trust him.

Anyone who lives by these core values and principles become strong pillars on which relationships rest and this makes you feel secure. What's a relationship anyway if it doesn't make you feel secure? It's empty, it's a vacuum.

Choose Character

Our attitudes and philosophies of life literally get so entrenched into our thoughts and feelings that they become our beliefs. Unlike animals, who live by instincts, humans can choose their thoughts and build their character. Each day, we can decide to reflect, review, and improve our lives to a higher level of conduct.

If through experience, we know a person's character, then we can also predict how a person is likely to behave in a particular set of circumstances or situations. The more proficiently we are able to judge and assess the character of a person, the easier it becomes for us to choose the people we want to associate with, personally, professionally and socially. By 'personally' I refer to those 'who we want to establish relationships with, including getting married to'. By 'professionally' I mean those 'who we want to work with'; and by 'socially' I mean those 'who we want to elect as our leaders'.

I don't know of any human being who does not have moral shortcomings. We all do. There is no human being who might not have done something wrong through an act of omission or commission. Does one such mistake or wrong act make a person dishonourable?

Unfortunately, many good people make mistakes and might commit some lapses inadvertently or out of weakness. The weakness may be momentary, but the consequences are permanent. It is always the first lapse which is difficult but after that it becomes a lot easier and we start justifying our behaviour. That is why it is so crucial to strive for ideals. The closer we get to them, the more honourable we become.

Ethical corporations have demonstrated both ethical and philanthropic values time and time again. For example:

1. *Readers' Digest* dropped cigarette advertising immediately when the surgeon general's warning came out that 'smoking causes cancer'. *Readers' Digest* lost millions in revenue, but they were committed to the well-being of their readership.
2. Andrew Carnegie, founder of US Steel, upon retirement in the early 1900s, gave close to half a billion dollars for public use in building schools, colleges and universities. He donated money to support education and help students carve their future.

> **The test of integrity comes only in the face of temptation. Till then, it is only speculation.**

I was staying at a five-star property called The Lalit, which was affiliated with the Intercontinental, Mumbai, at one point. Inside my suite, next to the bed, was a side table. On it was a digital clock, which looked aesthetically nice, but I would guess it was probably a couple of dollars and no more. Right next to that clock was a big sign that read, 'This clock is the hotel's property.' I started wondering why they had the need to put up that sign.

I asked this question to participants in my programme. I got all kinds of evasive answers without addressing the real issue, till one person got up and said that people steal. He further added, '*There are people who pay $400–500 for a room, per night, in a five-star hotel,* yet wouldn't think twice before picking up a digital clock, which may be worth only a couple of dollars.' Obviously, people who pay this kind of money for one night at a five-star hotel are not poor. They may be millionaires, multi-millionaires and possibly even billionaires. People habitually pick up crockery, cutlery and linen from hotels, and they think they are being smart rather than thieves. Many people even brag proudly in front their friends and family by saying, 'I collect souvenirs.' What kind of role models are they? What kind of poison are they spreading in society?

Justification of Unethical Behaviour

We often hear people say: 'So long as it is legal, who cares?' or 'We have to take business decisions, not ethical ones', or People justify, 'I am not as bad so long as, others are worse', or 'Where the culture is dishonest, an occasional liar stands out as honest'.

The justification of one's unethical behaviour is nothing but convenience of attitude. 'I'm basically honest' means 'occasional dishonesty' is OK.' When it is OK? When the price is right or the stakes are high. And what does that mean? It means either the risk is too deep or the profit is too lucrative, or both.

Well … the question is, is it ok?

True Character

With some people a lack of character becomes intrinsic.

Just like a donkey is a donkey, remains a donkey and dies a donkey.

> **A donkey remains a donkey no matter what he carries.**

- A donkey carrying a load of gold does not become a golden donkey.
- Similarly, a donkey carrying a bunch of diplomas and certificates does not become an educated donkey.
- A donkey roaming around a holy place carrying spiritual books does not become a spiritual donkey.

Warren Buffett said, *'Of the billionaires I have known, if they were jerks before they had money, they are simply jerks with a billion dollars.'*

Desperate Times

Why have trust and integrity become major topics today? We are living in desperate times — we desperately need people of character in all fields as there is an appalling dearth of them. We need people who cannot be bought or will not sell their soul in exchange for lucrative offers.

- Those who will honour their words.
- Those who will value character above wealth, whose integrity would not change with the amount involved.

- Those who would not compromise with the wrong, whose ambitions would not drive them to the point of selfishness, who would not justify the wrong by saying, 'everybody else is doing it'.
- Those who would not believe that deceit and conceit are qualities to succeed.
- Those who would have the courage to say no when the rest of the world says yes.
- Those who would value relationships greater than expediency and whose behaviour would not change with adversity or prosperity.

In other words, we need people **who have strength of character**.

Achievers Build Strength Of Character.

ACTION PLAN

- Evaluate your own life. In what three ways can you further build your character?

    i. _____

    ii. _____

    iii. _____

Success Without
Integrity Amounts
To Failure

────────────────────

CHAPTER 11

Integrity—A Way of Life

**" Integrity involves upholding
a personal moral code no matter
what the consequence. "**

Integrity means that 'we are uncorrupted and authentic'. People with integrity are not different things to different people. Their actions and words match. If we have a medical sickness and we go to the hospital, the doctors might have a disagreement on why we seem sick, but they are totally in agreement on what a healthy body looks like. The doctor might mistakenly send us with one limb less, but he will not send us with one additional limb.

Integrity matters. It impacts every area of our lives. It impacts all our relationships. Our friends are friends because we trust each other. They cease to be our friends when the trust goes missing. The trust factor gets dismantled the moment integrity is lost.

**Values are
Priceless** Integrity does not change with the amount involved.

We had a client enrolled into our leadership programme, who had to remit approximately Rs. 79,000 to us. By mistake, Rs. 11 million (approximately $300,000) was credited to our account. Our accountant took notice of this in the morning. After checking the balance, he came to my room and said in a light tone, *'We have become rich.'* I asked, *'How come?'* He said, *'One of our clients has sent us excess money by mistake to the tune of Rs. 11 million. I have double-checked the accounts and there is no confusion. It's a mistake on their part.'* He asked me what we should do with this money. *'Why are you asking me?'* I questioned.

Doesn't he know what is to be done with the money?

I asked him, *'What if I was travelling and not reachable, what should be done?'*

He said, *'We should double check the accuracy of the transaction, make sure we are not making a mistake otherwise that would become a bigger problem. We should inform the client and then instruct the bank to have the transaction reversed.'* We informed the client in Muscat, who worked at a two-hour time difference, about the incident and when they heard about it, there was panic at their end. We started getting calls, frantically. Our business head asked them, *'Why are you so frantic? First of all, we are the ones who have informed you, you were not even aware of it. And secondly, we need a couple of hours to give written instructions to our bank.'* After the transaction got reversed, we asked them, *'Why were you so frantic?'* They said, *'In this part of the world, the legal system doesn't work, in fact, nothing works. We were concerned if we will ever get the money, and if we do get it, when will we get it. You could hold it for years since the legal system doesn't work. Besides, the amount involved was on the higher side.'* We told them that our programmes are based on integrity and we make it a point to practise it in our office too. We have learnt one thing—integrity does not change with the amount involved. If it changes with the amount involved it only means we have no integrity, our price is different. It amounts to 'superficial integrity', which is up for sale if the price is right. On the lighter side, our business head mentioned to them that we may be stupid sometimes, but we are not crooked. We got a reply from them that read as:

> …We wish to acknowledge we have received back the excess amount mistakenly transferred by our bankers to your account and thank you and the entire Shiv Khera team for the prompt action…

> …We would once again like to place on record our sincere thanks on your prompt action.

Regards,

Shekar Subramanian
Manager – Finance & Systems
Al Hashar Pharmacy L.L.C., Muscat, Oman

Ethics   It's a myth that people in the business world say, 'We have to get real and it is the numbers and the profit that matter. Integrity does not come into play.' That's really not true. Ethical businessmen, who value their credibility, make decisions everyday based on integrity. They cannot do business with people they cannot trust.

After the 9/11 terrorist attack incident in the US in 2001, the stock market crashed. However, in 2002, it recovered. But around the same time, some major corporates like Enron and WorldCom went out of business only because of unethical reasons. In fact, because of some major corporate failures, due to unethical reasons the stock market crashed again, and this time even more than during the terrorist attack. What does that tell us? That the market feared unethical behaviour much more than terrorist attacks.

> *Moral collapse is a greater danger*
> *than a terrorist attack.*
> *Where morality collapses,*
> *men decay!*

The Question of Integrity Has Become Fundamental to All Professions

When we ask why does integrity matter? Then we need to also ask, what would happen when integrity fails? All relationships will fade away or die out. The basis of every relationship is trust. All relationships are **ethically and morally governed**. 'Can I trust you?' Becomes the most important question. Trust is the starting point. When a person's values and actions do

INTEGRITY – A WAY OF LIFE

not match, it amounts to hypocritical behaviour. Our integrity reveals our character, it reveals WHO WE ARE. This is the starting point of trust.

The integrity of a person is not measured by his status or profession, but by his conduct. It demands a clear-cut distinction between right and wrong. It requires moral courage in the pursuit of an ideal. Integrity combined with enthusiasm and determination makes for honourable living.

> *An upright person can never be a downright failure no matter what he does.*

Good Leaders Believe Strongly in Making Integrity a Way of Life

Abraham Lincoln was a very successful practising attorney. Once someone asked him to take up a case. After listening to the facts, Lincoln said, *'I understand your case. It's technically strong, but ethically weak. I cannot accept your case.'* Now the man said, *'I'm willing to pay your fees.'* Lincoln said, *'Fees is not the problem. The problem is that knowing the facts that I do, while I am arguing it in front of the judge, all the time, at the back of my mind, I'll keep saying to myself, "Lincoln, you're a liar. Lincoln, you're a liar." I will not be able to live with myself.'*

I interpret Lincoln's behaviour as, **'I sell my professional time, but not my conscience.'** My take-home is — **we sell products and services, we sell our**

professional time, but we don't sell our conscience.

Integrity fosters a feeling of security and confidence. A pillow of clear conscience affords the soundest sleep, and comes from a life lived with integrity. When a person tries to get out of a difficult situation through dishonest or unjust means, he really multiplies his problems till he reaches a point of no return.

On matters of integrity, remaining silent is a sign of weakness and cowardice. More lies have been told by **remaining silent**, when we **should have spoken**. Silence and integrity are two different things. Just because a person is silent does not mean that he has integrity.

> *Weak people can never be sincere and cowards can never practise morality.*

What is the Difference between Integrity and Honesty?

Integrity means 'having strong moral principles'. It is reflected in character, morality, virtues, fairness, ethics, and how upright and honourable one is.

Honesty is 'sincerity, truthfulness and freedom from deceit or fraud'.

Can a Person be Honest and Yet Not Have Integrity?

Integrity is a value system, whereas honesty or

dishonesty is a habit. People, who constantly practise telling the truth, get caught the first time they tell a lie. Reverse it. People, who constantly tell lies, get caught the first time they tell the truth. Can a person be honest and not have integrity? The answer is, yes.

For example, a teacher once asked a student, '*Son, if you found a wallet with a large amount of money, what would you do?*' The student replied, '*If no one was watching me, I would keep it.*' The teacher said, '*Son, you are honest, but you lack integrity.*' The student just demonstrated honesty by admitting to the teacher what he would do, but the choice of keeping the wallet that did not belong to him showed lack of integrity.

Can the Reverse be True as Well?

Could one not be honest and yet maintain integrity? Sometimes when racial riots break out, mobs come looking for innocent people to kill. If we give shelter to an innocent person and lie to the mob, that's being dishonest in words, but shows integrity in action. Would we rather be honest and have an innocent person killed? Is that integrity?

Supposing, I'm on my way to addressing a conference with a few hundred people and I run into Osama Bin Laden in the lobby. Osama asks me, '*I have some extra RDX with me and I would like to blow up a few hundred people. I believe you're having a conference around here. Can you tell me where is it?*'

Now, should I tell him the truth? Obviously not!

Caution: Undoubtedly, the above is an extreme case. What chance is there ever for me to meet Osama Bin Laden? None. Lying while maintaining integrity is a rare phenomenon — it does not happen every day. There are some people who are chronic liars and they justify their dishonest behaviour by saying, 'I am being diplomatic.'

Maintain and Sustain Integrity

Ancient wisdom says, 'Anything that is bought or sold has no value unless it contains the secret and the priceless ingredient which cannot be traded.' What is it? It is the credibility, the honour, and the integrity of the one who makes it. It is not such a secret, but it is priceless. The final product reflects the integrity of the person who has put his heart and soul into making it.

Let's look at another example of lack of integrity.

Three executives who were childhood friends were out on a personal lunch. When the bill came, they were fighting over who would pay the bill. One said, '*I will pay, I can get a tax deduction.*' The other said, '*Let me have it, I will get reimbursement from my company.*' The third said, '*Let me pay, because I am filing for bankruptcy next week.*'

Integrity demands that we should have the courage:

1. To say no to deceit
2. To face the truth
3. To do the right thing because it is right

Integrity and Values

Honesty and dishonesty are both learnt traits: Honesty and dishonesty are neither the domain of the prosperous nor the poor. Either could be honest or dishonest. People with low self-esteem have no problems in compromising their values for ulterior motives. People with integrity are driven more by the desire to do the right thing than by the desire not to get caught. Genuine honesty does not look for concealment or camouflage.

People who lack integrity believe honesty restricts them. In fact, it's the opposite. Honesty actually frees people from the fear of getting caught. It helps create an environment of trust.

Practise Integrity and Honesty

A person with high self-esteem would prefer not to transact anything in any relationship by telling lies. Why? Because, to him, his credibility is more important than the transaction. He will not put a price tag on his credibility. Validation of integrity should happen from within.

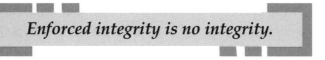

Enforced integrity is no integrity.

Trying to Rationalise the Wrong

Some people think it is really not considered stealing if the theft goes unnoticed, or if the other person has a surplus of something. Taking things that don't belong to us without permission, even with the intention of replacing them, is stealing.

It is a common practice that people take and keep things that do not belong to them, and rationalise their behaviour.

Once at a grocery store in New Jersey, I purchased a packet of disposable razors priced at $7.95. As I was passing through the cash counter, a clerk scanned the razor and the display read $11.95. Since, I had carefully noted the price, I told the clerk that there was a mistake and that the price should be $7.95. He double-checked his record and said, *'The correct price is $11.95.'* To resolve the issue, he called the manager who wanted to see where I had picked the pack of razors from. After seeing where the pack of razors was kept, and that it had been tagged at $7.95, he verified his records and said that it was mistakenly put on the wrong rack. The correct price was in fact $11.95. As I was checking out, I noticed that he had not charged me for the pack of razors. I asked him, *'Sir, there is a mistake in the bill, you have not charged me for the razors.'* The manager said, *'There is no mistake. It is our store policy that if the mistake has originated from the store, we give it complimentary.'* I said, *'It's an honest mistake and it can happen to anyone.'* I still offered to pay, *'Thank you for being so generous, but at least accept the price on the rack that is $7.95.'* He again politely refused to accept it. He said, *'It is our store policy that if the mistake has originated from the store, we give it complimentary. Please accept it.'*

I thanked him and left. I narrated this incident at a social get-together and to my utter disappointment and disgust, the first reaction I got from some of the people at the gathering was, *'Next time when I go to that store, I will take an item that is sitting on a higher-priced rack, put it on a lower priced rack, and possibly get away by not paying.'*

I have come to the conclusion that to a crook, only a crooked path looks straight.

Does this sound familiar? I'm sure it does!

This is **degradation of values.**

To some people, possession implies ownership. Just because I have it, doesn't mean it's mine. Going by the same analogy, keeping extra change given mistakenly by a cashier or not paying for a dish that the waiter forgot to put on the bill, seems justified. Forget being embarrassed, the dishonest people, in fact, feel proud to brag about it.

A similar instance that comes to my mind is that of a young girl who told her friends that she got a pair of shorts for free because the cashier made a mistake, and due to an oversight, did not charge for it. She did not feel any obligation to pay. Her thinking was, *'It was his fault. His mistake was my gain.'*

Let's analyse the repercussions of her behaviour. The repercussion didn't bother her. It could have only bothered her if she had a conscience — that alone would have raised many questions:

1. What if she was the cashier at the store?
   Answer: Possibly, she would have had to pay for
   it or could have even lost her job.

2. What if she was the owner of the store?
   Answer: She would have had to bear the loss.

3. What is to say that because she got away this time
   with the shorts, she will not repeat a similar or
   bigger act of dishonesty elsewhere?

4. Did she know what she put at stake?

5. Can she face herself in the mirror after what she
   did? Wouldn't she be carrying an excess baggage
   on her conscience?

No matter how we analyse it, stealing and cheating are
classified as dishonest. This situation doesn't really
call for any analysis. The answer is not complicated
—it's blatantly simple. An honest person with
integrity would have just gone back and returned the
shorts or paid for it.

Cost of Dishonesty It's common sense that stealing
from any establishment impacts its
profits adversely. The cost to replace
the stolen good also increases the selling price,
which eventually has to be paid by the consumer.
Additionally, there is a cost to prevent thefts, which
also eats into the profits.

- According to a survey conducted by the National
  Association of Shop Lifting Prevention, 'Product
  theft causes $13 billion in annual loses in

the US',[1] translating to approximately \$35 million/
day.

Here are a few other examples of stealing, cheating
and dishonesty:

- Stealing is not only robbing material goods, even
  leaking of confidential information of an employer
  to a competitor is stealing.
- False advertising is another form of stealing.
- Besides embezzlement, another example of
  stealing is taking office supplies home without the
  knowledge of the employer.
- Doing personal work in company time is another
  kind of stealing.
- Wasting time during working hours is stealing.
- Not paying what is due to others in time is stealing.
  Just because the culprit is not easily identified for
  stealing does not absolve him of his responsibility.
- Allowing children of an impressionable age to
  watch inappropriate movies robs them of their
  innocence – that's stealing.
- Falsifying documents at offices – for example, time
  sheet of employees coming in and out; lawyers,
  doctors and accountants billing for false hours,
  etc. – is stealing.
- Taking office documents or stealing data on thumb
  drives is stealing.
- A doctor conducting useless tests and surgeries is
  stealing.

---

[1] *http://smallbusiness.chron.com/stealing-affect-store-profit-37180.
html*

Different Creative Faces of Dishonesty Many times, we ignore the most obvious. Dishonesty has many faces. Crooks create some of the most innovative ways to be dishonest, to cheat and to steal.

Once a factory manufacturing many things including bags, was facing a theft problem. The management started to inspect the belongings and bags of all employees, but they found nothing. Yet the thefts continued. The question was, what were the workers stealing? Well, they were stealing the bags. This little scenario might sound hypothetical. The guards were so focused on checking the inside of the bag that they did not even pay attention to the fact that the most obvious thing being stolen was the bag itself. Many times it is assumed that the things that are stolen are hidden.

The obvious was overlooked.

At the Pearly Gates A lawyer died pretty young. At the mere age of thirty-five, he was standing at the Pearly Gates. He was rather angry and surprised as he had a long way to go on earth. Money was pouring in so fast that he lost count. So he asked God, *'I'm only thirty-five. How come you called me so fast? This is no age to die.'* God replied, *'We have checked our accounting department, and based on the hourly billing that you have done to your clients, it appears that you have exceeded the age of hundred.'* This might sound a little humorous but such things are happening in the real world. This lawyer proves the saying right—**a crooked lawyer with a briefcase can steal more than a hundred robbers with guns.**

Achievers Believe Strongly In Making Integrity A Way Of Life.

ACTION PLAN

- Write down three areas where you commit to overcome temptation to practise integrity:

    i. _____

    ii. _____

    iii. _____

- How will practising integrity improve your life?

    i. _____

    ii. _____

    iii. _____

A Champ or a Cheat?

Credibility Determines Profitability
A couple of years ago, I was addressing a few thousand people in Singapore. After I finished my speech, somebody asked me very pointed questions.

- Was Maradona a champ or a cheat?
- Was Lance Armstrong a champ or a cheat?
- Was Tiger Woods a champ or a cheat?

While I was about to answer, somebody from the audience volunteered to answer instead. I said, *'Go ahead.'* His answer was very short and crisp, *'They were all champs till they cheated or till they got caught.'* The answer has two components:

1. The first one means that 'they were champs but they ceased to be champs after they cheated. Getting caught was only incidental.'
2. The second half of the answer means that 'they were cheats, but this was the first time they ever got caught. So they weren't champs to begin with.'

The question still remains unanswered. Was it the first time they cheated or was it the first time they ever got caught? The truth may always remain a mystery.

Let us evaluate the consequences of such actions.

No doubt, **credibility determines our profitability**. But profitability is not the reason why we practise values. If we practise values because of profitability, we are acting. Then we should go to Hollywood or Bollywood. We practise values because we believe in them. That is the difference between **reputation** and **character**. Reputation is 'what other people think of us,' Character is 'who we know we are'; and they could be totally two different things. Some people are honest, because they don't want to get caught telling lies. They are doing the right thing for a wrong reason; whereas, some people are honest, because they believe it's the right thing to do. They are doing the right things for the right reason.

In all the examples below, there is no doubt that these famous personalities had built great reputations but compromised on character. They lost millions and millions in revenues. But as compared to the real loss, the financial loss was insignificant. What they lost was priceless. They lost their credibility. They lost respect.

1. Lance Armstrong

- According to *ESPN.in*, 'The decision by the International Cycling Union marked an end to the saga that brought down the most decorated rider in tour history and exposed wide spread cheating in the sport.'[1]

After the report from the United States Anti-doping Agency (USADA), all of Lance Armstrong's sponsors dropped him. The American former professional road-racing cyclist, Armstrong, in Cyclingnews.com, reportedly, lost $75 million in a day.

- According to *theguardian.com*, USADA's report on Armstrong, released in 2012, 'accused him of leading "The most sophisticated, professionalised and successful doping programme that sport has ever seen." UCI stripped him of his seven Tour De France titles and banned him for life. In 2013, the international Olympic Committee stripped him of the bronze medal he won at the 2000 Olympic Games in Sydney, Australia. In an interview with Oprah Winfrey, Armstrong admitted to using banned performance-enhancing drugs.'[2]

2. Diego Armando Maradona

- In 1991, Maradona, the famous football player, failed a drug test for cocaine, earning a fifteen month suspension from the sport. He was sent home from the 1994 World Cup after testing positive for a banned stimulant.[3]

---

[1] *http://www.espn.com/olympics/cycling/story/_/id/8536389/uci-agrees-strips-lance-armstrong-7-tour-de-france-titles*

[2] *https://www.theguardian.com/sport/2015/mar/09/lance-armstrong-cycling-doping-scandal*

[3] *http://english.ahram.org.eg/NewsAFCON/2017/131384.aspx*

- In the 1986 World Cup, Diego Maradona found a way past England's goalkeeper, Peter Shilton, to score a goal illegally with his 'Hand of God'. 'Tunisian referee, Ali Bennaceur, allowed the goal to stand amid furious protests from the England players, prompting a debate that still rages on today, over the use of referees from smaller nations in major matches.'[4]

The way I see it, it is not a 'smaller nation' issue, it is a big integrity issue. This raises questions over the integrity of not only Maradona, but of the referee as well.

3. Ryan Lochte

A US swimming star, twelve times Olympic medalist's loss went into millions of dollars because of the lying scandal. But most importantly, the biggest loss he suffered was the loss of his own self-esteem. He concocted and lied about being robbed. The worst was that, according to an article in Time.com, 'He was tagged as "the ugly American" and "the most embarrassing American Olympian". Lochte has always been known as a publicity hound. He's worn a stars-and-stripes grill on his teeth, had his hair coloured bluish blonde, and starred in a reality TV show. But now he's getting attention for all the wrong reasons.'[5]

---

[4] *https://af.reuters.com/article/sportsNews/idAFKCN0QN11 P20150818*

[5] *http://time.com/money/4459036/ryan-lochte-rio-olympics-scandal-endorsements/*

- Sponsors like Ralph Lauren, Speedo and many others withdrew their sponsorship.[6] What a disgrace!

Further, this is a typical example of why people do all that — to offset the feeling of inadequacy. They feel there is a void and they want to cover the insecurity.

4. Tiger Woods

Golfing legend Tiger Woods, one of the highest paid athletes and one of the greatest golfers in the world, was hit by a sex scandal and ensuing divorce case. According to *Forbes* he was the 'first athlete to earn a billion dollars.'[7]

As per *New York Post*, 'Tiger Woods was exposed as a "serial cheater". Tiger Wood's wife chased him out of the house with a golf club after learning he'd been unfaithful.'[8]

According to a study by researchers at the *UCDavis. edu*, '...shareholders of Nike, Gatorade and other Tiger Woods sponsors lost a collective $5–12 billion in the wake of the scandal involving his extramarital affairs. Before the scandal, Woods earned about $100 million a year in endorsement income, more than any other athlete.'[9]

---

[6] *https://www.usatoday.com/story/sports/olympics/rio-2016/2016/08/22/speedo-ends-sponsorship-ryan-lochte/89099284/*

[7] *https://www.forbes.com/2009/09/29/tiger-woods-billion-business-sports-tiger*

[8] *https://nypost.com/2013/11/24/the-night-tiger-woods-was-exposed-as-a-serial-cheater/*

[9] *https://gsm.ucdavis.edu/news-release/tiger-woods-scandal-cost-shareholders-12-billion*

5. Volkswagen (VW)

The Environmental Protection Agency (EPA) found that many VW cars being sold in America had faulty emission systems.

- Volkswagen Posts Deep Loss after Taking $18.28 Billion Hit on Emissions Scandal.[10]
- According to *bbc.com*, 'The German giant admitted cheating emission tests in the US.'[11]

6. Bill Clinton

- According to an article by *telegraph.co.uk* on 12 January 2003, Bill Clinton's candidacy as the chancellor of Oxford University faced growing opposition from dons who feared that his election would endanger the reputation of the institution and the virtue of its students. His lies on oath about the Lewinsky Affair and his decisions to award presidential pardons to well-connected criminals made him unfit for such a role.

  Dr Jeremy Catto, the senior Dean of Oriel College and a fellow in medieval history, said, 'Having Clinton as Chancellor wouldn't exactly add to the dignity of the office. Given his past record, I shouldn't think for a moment that the university's women students will be safe.' Mark Almond, a fellow of the Oriel College and a lecturer, added that Mr Clinton would face 'endless allegations of

---

[10] *https://www.wsj.com/articles/volkswagen-posts-deep-loss-after-taking-18-28-billion-hit-on-emissions-scandal-1461333307*

[11] *http://www.bbc.com/news/business-34324772*

sexual scandal. There's bound to be trouble.' He further added, **'We need a woman chancellor, not a womanising chancellor.'**[12]

For Achievers, Credibility Is Priceless.

12 Adapted from: *http://www.telegraph.co.uk/news/uknews/1418634/We-need-a-woman-chancellor-not-a-womanising-chancellor.html*

ACTION PLAN

Develop a High Standard of Personal Ethics

- Can you think of three instances when you have compromised your credibility?

    i. _____

    ii. _____

    iii. _____

- How did compromising credibility make you feel?

    i. _____

    ii. _____

    iii. _____

- Write down three things you commit to do to maintain your credibility:

    i. _____

    ii. _____

    iii. _____

Finding Balance

" There is a time for everything, and a
season for every activity under the heavens:
A time to be born and a time to die,
A time to plant and a time to uproot,
A time to kill and a time to heal,
A time to tear down and a time to build,
A time to weep and a time to laugh,
A time to mourn and a time to dance,
A time to scatter stones and
a time to gather them,
A time to embrace and a time to
refrain from embracing,
A time to search and a time to give up,
A time to keep and a time to throw away,
A time to tear and a time to mend,
A time to be silent and a time to speak,
A time to love and a time to hate,
A time for war and a time for peace. "
— *The Bible,* Ecclesiastes 3

Lady Isobel Barnett, the wife of Leicester's Lord Mayor, was highly successful and well respected. One day, she went to a department store to pick up a few things. She stole a tin of tuna and a carton of cream. She did this because she had an irrepressible urge to take away things without permission. She could not resist stealing and was caught on camera. Next day, the act became big news. She was painted black overnight. The humiliation faced was awful. Out of shame, she committed suicide. For a woman, like her, stealing such petty things was unimaginable; but she stole because her negative conditioning overtook her ethical behaviour. She was neither ignorant nor innocent; she was fully aware of her actions. She knew what she was doing was wrong. In medical terms, this irrepressible desire to steal is called kleptomania; but in my opinion, it is negative conditioning of the subconscious mind. We acquire false perceptions and if not corrected during the formative years, they become habitual.

Lady Barnett was respected and prosperous, and yet she committed suicide out of guilt. It was certainly an extreme act. She lost her balance. Giving into impulses may appear easy, but **striking a balance** is difficult.

In today's time, we all seem to be running fast—at times, too fast. Amid the countless social streams, we get pulled away from our centre. We need to find our centre again. How? By striking a balance.

Striking a If we fall while walking on grass,
Balance nothing happens, but if we fall from
a twenty-storeyed building while
walking on a tight rope, the game is over. Which
means, the higher we go in life, the greater is the
responsibility and the tougher it is to maintain
balance. One must maintain equilibrium. The higher
we tread in life, the more careful we need to be.

There are three kinds of people in this world:

1. **The ones with jawbones:** They are talkers and
   not doers. They talk ceaselessly, at times foolishly,
   and do nothing productive. Most of their talk is
   negative and pulls people down.

2. **The ones with wishbones:** They are dreamers,
   but not doers. These people always wish that
   others do their work. They keep passing the buck.
   They always keep wishing for things to happen,
   but never make things happen themselves.

3. **The ones with backbones:** They are doers and
   action-oriented. They have the guts to take
   calculated risks. They are the ones who make
   things happen, while maintaining a balance.

We need to strike a balance between family and
friends, home and work, earning and spending,
even sugar levels in our bodies—both too much or
too little are harmful. If we have two children—we
have to strike a balance between both. Even if we go
on a holiday, we have to have a balance. Finding a
balance between intangibles in life is easy, but finding
a balance between the following can be tricky and
delicate:

- Emotions and logic
- Relations and commitments
- Gentleness and strength

These are things that we do not learn in schools and colleges out of academic books. 'Laws of emotion' are not like the laws of gravity — they aren't standard across the world. One plus one may not always be two in the laws of emotion, it can vary from three, four, five, and ten or even go into the negative. While talking of emotions, digits can ebb and flow. That's why we need to strike a balance with respect to our family, work, society, emotions and relations.

Our health depends on the balance of our body. A building needs balance to stand firmly. Balance in life is very important. We need to strike a balance between our aspiration and inspiration. Sometimes, people become over ambitious and self-destruct. In fact, without balance in the cosmos, everything will self-destruct. You can understand this by looking at our solar system — the earth keeps rotating on its own axis due to which we have twenty-four hours, a day, and a night. If the speed of rotation changes by even a fraction, things would go topsy-turvy. We would not have days and nights then, but disasters and nightmares. Balance in nature keeps us functioning properly. Look at the ecological balance — when glaciers melt due to global warming, floods bring disaster by submerging countries and drowning people.

A Balanced Mind

A disordered mind can cause catastrophes. Imagine that we need a brain surgery. Who would we look for? Obviously, the best surgeon in town — not the second or the third best, unless we have no choice. How do we know he is the best? We check out his credentials — his qualifications and track record. We figure it out by looking at the wall full of his certificates, testimonials, and pictures. We know his credibility by the surgeries he has done on some of the greatest celebrities in the world. Maybe, he has performed some of the most complicated surgeries too and everybody in town refers to him as the best. It is beyond doubt that he is the best, so we readily agree for the surgery. Supposing, right before going into the operation theatre, the nurse comes and whispers into our ears, *'The doctor lost his wife last night. Since this morning, we've all noticed that he has lost his balance. Somehow, he doesn't appear to be himself.'*

Now, would we get our surgery done by him? Probably not! Why, what has changed?

- His credentials haven't
- His qualifications haven't
- His track record hasn't
- His experience hasn't
- His credibility hasn't

But we don't want to be operated by him, because we are not sure of his mental and emotional balance. A balanced mind is more important than all the degrees, qualifications, knowledge, and experience put together. This story may be imaginary but the message is real. What is required to succeed in life is — **mental and emotional balance**.

Insight is More Important Than Eyesight

We get stuck in traffic, we lose our cool. Who is controlling us? Our mind is, but its balance is shaken. When the weather changes outside, we get disturbed internally and emotionally. Our balance is disturbed. We see things around us, but often forget things inside us.

We are living in a world of remote controls.

- When a person cuts across our car foolishly, and we get mad and become emotionally imbalanced, who has the remote? The other person has it. If similar things happen twenty times a day, then twenty times we hand over our remote control to somebody else.
- We go to buy something and the cashier messes up at the shop. We get mad — we give our remote control to the cashier. If we have to wait for a few extra minutes, we get mad and give out one more remote control.
- Our laundry man messes up our trousers. We get mad and give another remote control to the laundry man.
- We go to a get-together and somebody says they do not like us, and we pass on another remote control to them.

The above are examples of loss of mental balance.

The moral is very clear — they are all real life issues

and we cannot live in denial, but we must not keep handing over our remote controls to other people. We cannot allow others to operate on us or influence us to the extent that we lose control over ourselves, disruptively. We shouldn't allow life to let us drift. We need to become a general of our own army. If we want to test our mental strength, we should count:

- How many times in a day do we get emotionally disturbed?
- How many things disturb us every day?
- What are the kind of things that disturb us every day?

The more such things disturb us, the greater number of times we hand over our remote controls and grow weaker. This just means that we need to be self-aware and in control of our mental and emotional balance.

> *Not only do we have to be a careful driver, but we also have to be careful and protect ourselves from careless drivers.*

We don't drink and drive; but we definitely have to protect ourselves from drunk drivers. That's how we save ourselves from emotional pulls.

Out of Syllabus!   Not all imbalances in life are self-generated. Many times, students complain of out-of-syllabus questions in examinations. When students keep complaining about such things, they actually imply that they have the right to fail. Remember, in life, many situations arise that are 'out-of-syllabus' in the real world. We have to be guided by a moral compass, which has nothing to do with the syllabus. Once we clear our academic education, we have to go through life dealing with everything out-of-syllabus.

When we get married, do we have a checklist or a syllabus? Obviously not. When we get married, the extended family comes along with the union. Many times, we need and possibly even want to interact with them. Do they come with a syllabus? Which syllabus can one work with? None. By and large, we find that it is only the person, who is not prepared is the one who complains of the questions being out-of-syllabus.

Sometimes, even with the best balance, things may still go wrong and we may be put to test. After a hectic day at work, you go home and find something wrong with your neighbour. You see he has left his overflowing trashcan open right in front of your main door. The foul smell is unbearable, and in addition, it has already started inviting flies and insects. A test of balance may be waiting for you. What do you do? Do you go knock his head off or think about a scenario that solves the problem of foul smell and infection without meddling with your inner peace? The appropriate way is to politely make your neighbour aware of the risks both the families are exposed to. The second way is to just call up the authority at the building and let them address the situation instead of you running into a heated argument, a head-on collision with your neighbour. Now let's take it a step further. What if the authorities fail to remedy the situation? There could be many more multiple 'what ifs' that still may be beyond your control. What do you do then? Eventually, it all boils down to 'should we maintain a balance' or 'should we lose our cool?' Maintaining balance puts us in charge, we are in control no matter what, and our decision-making ability is a lot better. Whereas, if we lose our cool, we become emotionally disturbed and our decision-making ability gets distorted. No matter what the situation in life is — the key is to maintain INTERNAL BALANCE.

> *To achieve more not only requires presence of balance, but also overcoming imbalance.*

Life is a Matter of Stability and Balance! All great achievements of our life depend on the health of our minds.

There is a story of a wealthy person who had hundreds of acres of land, a huge mansion, and rare collectibles from around the world. One day, he called a spiritual teacher and started showing him around his beautiful huge mansion.

After he almost finished showing around the mansion, he took the teacher to the last room where there was a young boy locked in a cage. The teacher was rather shocked and in surprise, he asked the rich man, *'Why have you put this boy in this cage like a wild animal. Who is he?'* The rich man replied, *'He is my only son and the heir to everything I own in this world, but is mentally unstable. We have given him the best medical aid in the world but to no avail.'* The teacher said, *'But he's your only son.'* The rich man said, *'I know it, but he doesn't know he's my only son.'* Then the teacher pointed out an observation he had made, *'The help is enjoying all the wealth of this home much more than your heir.'*

This brings us to understand that the **strength of mind is more crucial than wealth and riches**.

> *Stability of mind is more important than education, wealth or even status.*

Let's look at another example.

Margaret Thatcher was considered to be the 'Iron Lady'. She was highly respected. When she spoke, the world listened. That was the strength of this lady. This was her power, but unfortunately, before she died, she was suffering from Parkinson's disease. She couldn't meet or recognise anybody. She didn't know what she said or to whom. She had lost her mental stability. The once prime minister of the UK, the most powerful lady, became a 'nobody' since she lost the stability of her mind.

It would not be out of line to say that US is the most affluent and powerful country in the world and that the most powerful person in the world is its President. Yet, according to the American constitution, if it can be proven by an appropriate body that the president of the US is mentally ill or unstable, he can be removed. Stability of mind is the most powerful quality of any person in the world, regardless of position and education. When the most powerful people in the world need stability, don't we all need it too?

Plato rightly said, 'Self conquest is the greatest of victories.'

Are We Victims of Public Success and Private Failure?

A man went to a psychiatrist and said, '*I have a suicidal tendency. I always feel depressed. I don't want to live. I want to commit suicide.*' The doctor checked him out, conducted all tests and said, '*I can't find anything wrong with you. I can make you a suggestion, take it as a prescription. There is a circus going on in town. Why don't you go there twice a day? I'm sure you will really enjoy yourself and have a good time as they have a clown who makes you laugh hysterically. He is really funny and has a great sense of humour. You will come out laughing and feeling on top of the world. Whenever I feel low, I go there too just to laugh and come back in high spirits.*' The man replied, '*Doctor, I have a very different problem, I am that clown.*' This is a prime example of achieving success publically, but failing privately, and it is called public success but private failure.

Dr John Gray, the author of *Men are from Mars and Women are from Venus*, has helped many families from breaking down and has brought them together. But, unfortunately, he himself got divorced.[1] Here was a person who was teaching and preaching about maintaining positive relationships that he himself was not able to sustain. In absence of facts, I am not in a position to point a finger, but perhaps just highlight a contradiction! Again, an example of public success and private failure.

Many times, we fall into the trap of maintaining a lifestyle, which gives us public success but private failure. That's why it is crucial to probe inwards and 'know thyself'. Many scriptures say the same thing. We must master the world inside before we master the world outside.

When internal contentment is missing, external success means nothing. Success is an experience, it's a feeling. We cannot make anyone feel successful. The feeling must come from within. That is why many times what appears to be success externally may be total emptiness internally. No wonder celebrities and billionaires who were considered successful such as Elvis Presley, Marilyn Monroe and Michael Jackson either took drugs and/or committed suicide. The world considered them successful, but they felt empty inside. These are some examples of public success but private failure. Success without fulfilment is empty. It's like good looks without goodness. We must have

---

[1] *Fact derived from https://www.marsvenus.com/john-grays-life-story.htm*

Private Success substance over form, not form
Public Failure over substance.

Most people know of the Wright brothers who invented the aircraft. As per Wikipedia, however, what most people don't know is that the aircraft was actually invented before the Wright brothers by Dr Stephen Langley and it took its first successful flight in 1896. Most people were sceptical post its meeting with an accident on 8 December 1903. Langley, probably disheartened, dumped his machine in the warehouse. He died heartbroken. Only a few days later, the Wright brothers made their first successful flight on 17 December 1903. The tragic part was that the very flying machine Dr Langley had made and dumped was flown by Mr Glenn Curtis successfully in 1914. Unfortunately, Dr Langley could never achieve public success.

So it is clear from these instances that a balance needs to be maintained to enjoy both public and private success.

We keep looking to take charge of the external world, while many a times forgetting to control the inner world. The inner world is more important than the outer world. We see things not the way they are, but the way we are. It is well said that the greatest mistake is of the one who sees everything around him but forgets to look inside himself.

Let's ponder over a question—what is our typical concept of success? Maybe, we want to be the chairperson, the country head, or the CEO of a multimillion-dollar organisation. Take a look at the example of Buddha who was born a prince and had a great kingdom. He had everything in the world, but eventually left it all, winning everyone's heart around the world. Today, how many people have the amount of influence that Buddha has? Hardly any! He inquired into his inner world to get answers — he made his own discoveries. All of us don't have to be the Buddha nor can we become the Buddha. However, we've got to preserve balance, cultivate mental peace, and then aim for worldly success. That is what can bring us inner happiness. *People say we cannot change the world, but who says that we cannot change ourselves?* We keep looking for the path to happiness not realising that happiness is the path.

Achievers Maintain A Balance Between What They Can Do And What They Cannot Do. They Live Between Fate And Free Will.

ACTION PLAN

- Stability of mind depends on how you handle challenging situations. On a scale of 1–10 (1 being poor control and 10 being excellent control), how many times in a day do you lose control at:

  i. Work _____ | 1 | 2 | 3 | 4 | 5 | 6 | 7 | 8 | 9 | 10 |

  ii. Home _____ | 1 | 2 | 3 | 4 | 5 | 6 | 7 | 8 | 9 | 10 |

  iii. Children _____ | 1 | 2 | 3 | 4 | 5 | 6 | 7 | 8 | 9 | 10 |

  iv. Traffic _____ | 1 | 2 | 3 | 4 | 5 | 6 | 7 | 8 | 9 | 10 |

  v. Others _____ | 1 | 2 | 3 | 4 | 5 | 6 | 7 | 8 | 9 | 10 |

  This calculation will give you an estimate of how many times you hand over your remote control to someone else. Assess and evaluate.

- Write down three ways you plan to maintain mental and emotional balance:

  i. _____

  ii. _____

  iii. _____

- From the above evaluation, write down three commitments that you will practise for the next thirty-one days to stay in control.

  i. _____

  ii. _____

  iii. _____

It Is Much Easier
To Do The Right Thing
The First Time,
Every Time, Than To
Explain Why We
Didn't And Correct
It Later

CHAPTER 14

Pride in Performance

" *People who take pride in their
performance, take ownership,
and hold themselves accountable to
much higher standards than others do.* **"**

**What is the
Sign of a Good
Professional?**
We all have our good days
in life and we all have our
bad days. There are days when
we wake up in the morning
feeling good. The world looks nice, productivity goes
up, and relationships are a lot better, no matter what
we do comes easy. There are days when we wake up
not feeling good and no matter what we do, it takes a
lot out of us.

What is the sign of a good professional? The sign of a
good professional is that on a good day or a bad day,
his performance remains identical. On a good day, it
comes easy. On a bad day, it takes a lot out of him,
but he does not compromise on performance.

Many times, professionals such as singers and speakers get booked a year in advance. How do they know that the night before the performance they may or may not run a 104° fever? And once in a while, they even do. But the next day, when they get on the stage to perform, they don't tell their audience that their performance would not be as good because they are running a fever. They don't say anything, they just perform to the same level of excellence and the audience never gets to know. Their self-esteem does not let them falter. There is a tremendous correlation between self-esteem and performance. People with high self-esteem perform no matter what, even when it hurts. Their self-esteem makes them push beyond their comfort zone and makes them excel.

It's worth repeating that **achievers don't compromise on performance. On a good day, it comes easy. On a bad day, it takes a lot out of them.**

> *We cannot justify poor quality and bad behaviour on grounds of expediency or speed.*
>
> *Three greatest enemies of progress are ignorance, incompetence, and indifference.*

Performers Look for Excellence and Not Perfection

Perfection is an elevated goal in life. It invariably remains out of reach.

- A perfect picture has never been painted.
- A perfect symphony has never been composed.

Perfection is an illusion. However, in the pursuit of perfection, we end up attaining excellence.

Never settle for anything less than excellence— excellence is a way of life.

Aristotle said, 'Excellence is not an act but a habit.'

> *Excellence cannot be achieved without taking pride in performance.*
>
> *People who are habitually quality conscious can never produce mediocre results.*

People, who take pride in performance, do the right thing out of passion, not compulsion. They are committed to excellence. Every person who is committed to doing the best does not start a revolution, but surely makes a positive contribution.

When we don't meet standards, there are two choices—either we increase our efforts to meet the grade or lower our benchmarks. If we choose to lower our benchmarks, degradation seeps in. The question is—why would we compromise to lower the standards? It is because we accept degradation as a way of life and think the pain is not worth the gain.

The more we compromise on our benchmarks,

the greater is the degradation and damage. High performers increase their efforts to meet the grade.

People who take pride in performance have a few particular attributes:

1. They stand for quality. Excellence becomes their hallmark.
2. They set higher benchmarks for themselves.
3. They hold themselves accountable for results.
4. They always give more than what they get.
5. They are engrossed in continuous learning.
6. They strive for continuous improvement.
7. They are self-motivated and endeavour to do the right thing first time, every time.
8. They are result oriented. They deliver no matter what.

> *A good craftsman measures twice before cutting. A bad one constantly blames his tools.*

Pride in Errors It's a practice in our office that whenever we hire people, we give the candidate a short dictation without really rushing him. Only once he is completely through and satisfied with his assessment do we take a printout of the dictation. We then take note of the red underlined texts. Obviously, it's red either because of a spelling or a spacing mistake. In that case we ask him, *'Why is that red line showing?'* He says, *'Oh, I forgot to spell check.*

Normally, I do it but today I thought you are in a rush...'
The question is, if a person normally spell checks why
wouldn't he do it this time? Is he stating the truth?
We gave him sufficient time without rushing him,
so obviously it's clear that he normally doesn't spell
check. So if we're hiring him, what are we doing? We
are inviting trouble.

We close the interview right then and there. It's
a very simple derivation—if he took pride in his
performance, would he not spell check? Would he not
want to deliver a draft without errors? A person who
has come for a job interview is obviously looking to
get selected. If this is his best foot forward, can you
imagine what his worst would be? This person takes
pride in errors and not in performance.

Such corrections are a matter of just a few seconds.
People who take pride in performance, never ever
lower their standards nor accept anything short of
excellence. It is the commitment to excellence that
builds the reputation of being a quality person who
delivers quality output.

Only Quality People Deliver Quality Output

Only when we consistently deliver quality do we
gain credibility, respect, and admiration. Most of the time, life
gives us four choices—poor, fair, good and excellent.
How high we go up in life will depend on what we
choose. Someone once said, '**Every job is a self-portrait of the person who does it. Autograph your work with excellence.**'

Once a great Danish sculptor was asked, *'What do you consider your best statue?'* Without a second thought, he replied, *'It is yet to come.'*

A top-notch athlete was ready to compete. He seemed rather nervous. Somebody asked him, *'Why are you so nervous?'* His answer was, *'To compete with others I have to put in 100 per cent, but to stay top notch I have to put in 150 per cent.'*

To attain the status of being top notch in any field, one must put in 150 per cent.

People with pride in performance always put their heart into whatever they do.

> **People with pride in performance don't work for recognition, but do work which is worthy of recognition.**

Attempt with No Intent

Think of a commonly practised scenario.

Suppose we tell our secretary to convey a message to a client and we provide him the client's number as well. We give clear instructions on what ought to be done, and we also tell him to let us know if he runs into any problem. The secretary confirms that he has understood the instructions and can easily handle it. He accepts to finish the work. As far as we are concerned, this task is considered done and, mentally, we feel relieved. Suddenly, a week later, as we are passing by the corridor, we ask our secretary if the task was done and he replies, *'It wasn't.'* We ask, *'Why?'* and the answer is, *'I tried the number, but couldn't get through.'* We ask, *'Then what did you do?'* The answer we get is, *'Nothing.'*

If we analyse the above scenario, the recipient of the task neither did the work nor informed us about the work not being done. We weren't even told that he ran into a roadblock. He did nothing. However, he did make the first call all right and stopped. The questions that arise here are:

1. Is this responsible behaviour?
2. Did he have the intent to do the job?
3. If he had the intent to do the job, and if he ran into a problem, would he not inform us and seek help?
4. He neither did the job nor informed us. What is this called? How do you classify this issue? Is it:

   i. Mistake
   ii. Negligence
   iii. Bad Attitude
   iv. Carelessness
   v. Oversight
   vi. Discipline issue
   vii. Integrity

What was missing in the above example?

   i. Accountability
   ii. Responsibility
   iii. Ownership
   iv. Intent

As a matter of fact, it is all of the above and can be summed up as **ATTEMPT WITH NO INTENT.** In the above example, the secretary was professionally qualified to do the job but he didn't. *We are responsible both for our actions and inactions. A person who attempts without the intent, quits at the first obstacle.* **Professional qualifications do not necessarily make a professional — one needs more than professional qualifications to be a professional.** *The difference between an honest mistake and a crooked one is the intent.*

Only whole-hearted effort gives results. The keyword here is 'whole-hearted'. Half-hearted efforts do not give half-hearted results; they give negative or damaging results. Often, you may have heard people say, 'I'll give it a shot' or 'I'll try'. What they are really saying is that, 'they'll attempt it, if it works fine, if it doesn't, they will quit'. In fact, subconsciously, they have planned to quit even before they begin. They are starting from a non-committal mindset and it reflects in their behaviour. It's a guaranteed failure. They'll run at the first sign of a problem.

> *People keep looking for job security not realising that the greatest job security is performance.*
>
> ————◦————
>
> *On the other hand, people who just look for security without responsibility, miss great opportunities.*

Everybody hits roadblocks and removing roadblocks is what a person is engaged to do. **If we don't remove the roadblocks, then we are the roadblocks.**

In life, results are rewarded, efforts are not. We judge ourselves by our intentions but the world judges us by our actions. People are not paid for their good intentions but for their **good actions**. There is an old saying, 'The road to hell is paved with good intentions.' **A small good action is better than a great intention. Good intentions are not good enough. They need to be supported with good actions.** What we think or believe is of little consequence. The only thing that counts is what we do.

We cannot climb a hill just by looking at it. People's abilities are measured by what they finish, not by what they attempt. The sad part of human life is that many people aspire to do things but very few actually tap their abilities. A little ability well used is much better than much ability unused.

We all have a list of things we must do — assignments, jobs, errands, etc. Most people do just enough to get by with. Yet satisfaction only comes from going the extra mile. **Life is like goalkeeping. It is not important how many goals we saved. Winning or losing depends on how many we missed.**

> *If we want to stand out then*
> *we need to do something outstanding.*

Star performers are result-oriented. They don't make excuses. They never say:

1. **'I thought everyone knew about it':** This is a typical response of non-performers to ensure that no one considers them accountable.

2. **'I thought someone else was going to do it':** This is a great justification for inaction. A responsible person should ask questions to keep things moving on track.

3. **'No one ever asked me to do it' or 'no one ever told me about it':** People who talk like this are operating with blinders or with a tunnel-vision, totally oblivious of what's going on around them.

4. **'They were supposed to get back to me' or 'they did not get back to me' or 'they are going to get back to me soon':** All these responses are a total demonstration of lack of responsibility. Why? Because, expecting someone else to get back to us puts us at their mercy and stops the action from our side. This is what people do when they do not want to take the initiative but only pretend involvement.

5. **'I just had no time' or 'I have been up to my neck':** When people keep saying such things, often, it is time to evaluate if they are worth retaining as their intent comes into question.

6. **'I did not think of that' or 'I did not think that it was important to ask those questions':** Such phrases show the inability or unwillingness of people to see beyond their nose and to grasp what is coming.

All of the above are so-called roadblocks that put a person's intent into question.

Achievers say I must do something, non-achievers say something must be done. Achievers act. Non-achievers react.

Pride in performance is not an event, it is an attitude. It impacts the quality of output in every area of our lives such as relationships, work, and social contributions.

Achievers Realise Pride
In Performance Is Not An Act
– It Is A Way Of Life.

ACTION PLAN

- Make your own list of dos and dont's. List three actions that you would take to make pride in performance a way of life and three actions you would abstain from:

Dos

    i. _____

    ii. _____

iii. _____

Dont's

    i. _____

    ii. _____

iii. _____

CHAPTER 15

Accidents are No Accidents

Casual Attitude Leads to Casualties

For want of a nail a kingdom was lost—this is a story about how a kingdom saw its downfall by someone's sheer negligence. In the mid-fifteenth century, King Richard was facing one of the toughest battles of his life. The King had a strong army and they were all prepared to defeat the enemy. He asked for his favourite horse to lead the troops. The blacksmith had shoed all the horses, but ran out of iron to shoe the King's main horse. They had no time to wait as the enemy was advancing. Eventually, the blacksmith fixed the shoe but could not guarantee that it would hold without the complete set of nails. King Richard's horse was not prepared. The armies clashed and in the thick of the battle, the King kept encouraging his troops. He galloped forward but barely had he gone a little distance when his horse's shoe fell off, the horse stumbled and King Richard was thrown to the ground. The frightened animal ran away and the

King was without a horse. His soldiers, unable to see their king, became demoralised and started running away too. Very soon, he was captured and the battle was over. What a shame! **Only because of the want of a nail, history changed forever.** Imagine the far-reaching impact of a nail. In the words of Benjamin Franklin, *'For want of a nail, a shoe was lost; for want of a shoe, a horse was lost; for want of a horse, a battle was lost; for want of a battle, a kingdom was lost and all for the want of a horse shoe nail.'*

The above is a true story with numerous questions and lessons.

1. Who was accountable for the missing shoe nail? Obviously, it was not the horse!
2. Was the king aware that his horse was not prepared?
3. And if he was why didn't he swap his horse with someone else's?
4. Or, was the king lied to, to believe that his horse was prepared?
5. The question is — was he really prepared?
6. If he was prepared, how come they did not have all the equipment and supplies?
7. How come they did not have all the iron to shoe all the horses?

All of this boils down to:

1. **Integrity**
2. **Responsibility**
3. **Accountability**
4. **Ownership**
5. **Casual attitude**

Somewhere, the casualty took place because of someone's casual attitude.

Was it only the blacksmith who messed up?

What about his supervisor, and all the supervisors above him and what about the General?

Finally, what about the King himself?

This means that multiple people goofed up. Their casual and laid-back attitude had such a disastrous consequence. Had anyone in the chain of command done their job right, this consequence could have been avoided. The king's army was strong and they were almost prepared. But lost!

The two important lessons here are:

1. **Almost prepared is not prepared.**
2. **We are only as strong as our weakest link.**

> ### Remember:
> *The difference between doing right and doing almost right is the same as the difference between being dead and almost dead. 'Almost' is not good enough. Nobody at the Olympics gets a gold medal for 99 per cent achievement.*
>
> ———
>
> *Almost done is not done. There is no such thing known as almost a century.*

Avoid Casualty Once a ticket checker got into a train and began inspecting tickets from the passengers. When he saw the ticket of the first passenger, he discovered that the passenger had the wrong ticket. The checker said, *'I am sorry Sir, you've taken the wrong train. You will have to change at the next station.'* Then he went further. He collected some more tickets and found that each of the passengers were carrying the wrong tickets. He was surprised to see so many people making the same mistake, until he realised the truth that he himself was on the wrong train. He was checking everybody's tickets not realising that he hadn't checked if he was on the right train. Don't we face similar situations in life when we realise that it isn't life that has created the problem, but that we ourselves are looking at life through the wrong end of the telescope. We are the problem.

Before looking for answers, we need to ascertain that we have the right questions. The greatest ignorance is when one is not aware of one's ignorance.

Duty Before Ritual Once, a group of tourists was going on a vacation to a mountain top. At the foothills, when everybody got into the bus, the tourists noticed that the driver went to the front of the bus, and with folded hands prayed for a few minutes. Thereafter, they started the climb up hill. Less than half way through, the engine started overheating so the driver had to stop the bus. When he checked he found that there was no water in the radiator. They got the situation rectified and started the journey onwards. Just a little distance later, the bus stalled and stopped right in the middle of the road. This time, it was because it ran out of fuel and the fuel tank was empty. Help came and the passengers were rescued.

The driver had said his prayers, but did not do what he was supposed to do — he had not checked the radiator nor had he filled the tank with fuel. He did not do his due diligence. What good would his prayers do when he hadn't done all that he was supposed to?

The moral of the above story is — **duties and responsibilities cannot be replaced by rituals.**

> *God does not help those*
> *who don't help themselves.*

The ticket collector's example might sound a little exaggerated, but the bus driver's example is not fiction but a reality of life. The bus driver cannot claim ignorance. The only behaviour he demonstrated is indifference. And what is indifference? It is a non-caring attitude. And what is non-caring attitude? It is a casual attitude. **A casual attitude always leads to casualty.**

> *Casualties can be caused due to*
> *multiple reasons. However, the major*
> *cause is indifference or apathy.*

Once a lady took her three-year-old daughter to a doctor with severe pain in her ear. The doctor diagnosed an ear infection and realising that the little girl would find it difficult to swallow pills, prescribed a syrup in a bottle with a dropper to the mother and said, *'Please give ten drops five times a day.'* The mother understood and said, *'OK,'* and went away satisfied. Two days later, the girl was rushed to the emergency. The doctor who gave the prescription was called for consultation. The doctor asked the mother if she had given ten drops five times a day as prescribed. The mother said, *'Yes.'* The doctor asked, *'How did you give it?'* The mother said, *'I gave ten drops five times a day in the ear.'* The doctor was shocked to hear this and said, *'I gave you the drops to be used orally, only because I realised the girl would have a problem swallowing pills.'*

Look at the miscommunication in this real life situation. Who is at fault? Who ought to be responsible for this casualty? Obviously, the above is a clear case of miscommunication. What caused the miscommunication? It was the casual attitude of both the doctor and the mother, who did not behave responsibly to clarify the instructions. Neither did the doctor instruct properly nor did the mother question the instructions to clarify.

A very clear case of casual attitude leading to casualty.

- According to *Washington Post*, dated 3 May 2016, 'A third leading cause of deaths (quarter million) that take place in the US are due to medical errors and negligence of the doctors and nurses.'[1]

Giving wrong medication, removing wrong body parts or miscommunication while handing patients from one department to another are examples of negligence.

A father while going to work in the morning noticed a bottle of medicine lying on the table with the cap open. The first thought that came to his mind was, why was the bottle open, and the second was, let me shut it. But he looked at his watch and realised he was running late. Without addressing the situation, he left. His wife was also busy in the kitchen doing chores. A few hours later, he got a call from his wife, who had taken their son to the hospital in a critical condition, stating that the child had died. The cause of death was over dosage of lethal medicine left open, carelessly.

The father could and should have behaved responsibly by putting the medicine beyond the reach of the child. And if not that, then he should have informed his wife to do so on his way out of the home. But in this case, considering what was at stake, informing the wife was also not the right thing to do, as possibly it could have slipped out of her mind. He should have done it himself as a priority.

Another real-life situation of casual attitude leading to casualty.

---

[1] *https://www.washingtonpost.com/news/to-your-health/wp/2016/05/03/researchers-medical-errors-now-third-leading-cause-of-death-in-united-states/?utm_term=.e526ed067be1*

There are more examples from daily life to show that indifference can lead to causalities. For example:

1. Mothballs are left in the open at homes. Children find them attractive and can pop them into their mouths. It could be fatal.
2. Electrical sockets are usually kept uncovered at homes, which can lead to casualties. To make them childproof, they should be covered.
3. People usually jump red lights to reach their destination faster, inviting causality.
4. Even governments act negligently when they leave potholes or manholes on the roads uncovered for pedestrians to fall in and die.

In all the above cases, the tragedies were avoidable only if the attitude was correct and responsible. Acceptance of their responsibilities could have saved casualties from occurring. **Ownership of responsibility** is what the world needs.

Accidents are No Accidents Mark Twain once said, *'It is better to be careful hundred times than to get killed once.'* Consider the statistics that eight out of ten accidents take place not because of unsafe conditions, but because of unsafe actions of the persons involved. Whenever accidents take place, the most common tendency is to look for scapegoats. At that time, people look for 'who to blame' rather than looking for the root cause. I am sure we all have been guilty of such an attitude or behaviour in our lives. If we continue with the same attitude, we may not be as lucky as we've been in the past.

A typical example of violating the safety norms is texting or talking on a mobile phone while driving. Texting while driving is like drinking and driving. What an open invitation to an accident! 'Every year in the U.S. approximately half a million people are injured or killed in traffic accidents because of texting and driving.'[2] No wonder, many countries have banned the use of mobile phones while driving.

- According to *Dailymail.co.uk*, 'Drivers are more distracted than ever before — and taking your eyes off the road for just two seconds increases accident risk by 24 times.'[3]

Those two seconds are long enough for a vehicle travelling at fifty-five miles an hour to cover the distance close to two football fields. It is like driving with a blindfold.

The following attitude leads to casualty:

1. **Lack of concentration:** Distractions can lead to accidents. Absent-mindedness, thinking of home while at work and work while at home destroys proper actions on both sides. Dragging on a problem or brooding over something bad that happened leads to lack of concentration and

---

[2] *https://www.personalinjurysandiego.org/topics/facts-about-texting-driving/*

[3] *http://www.dailymail.co.uk/sciencetech/article-3000917/Drivers-distracted-taking-eyes-road-just-2-seconds-increases-accident-risk-24-times.html*

causes accidents. We must learn to put a stop. Distractions or taking eyes off even to respond to a friendly social call may lead to an accident.

2. **Failing to follow safety procedures:** An indifferent attitude or a non-caring attitude could endanger people's lives. Casual attitude about safety procedures can lead to casualty. Ignoring safety procedures is a bad attitude. This is not innocence, it is indifference. For instance, people don't wear safety belts in the car.

3. **Ignoring or incomplete instructions:** Haven't we seen a person in our office being asked to do a task, but given only incomplete instructions? Such behaviour only compromises safety and output. The receiver should always ask and clarify instructions. It is not foolish to ask questions; it is always foolish to start a task without instructions.

4. **Complacence or over-confidence:** Over-confidence brings arrogance. It brings the attitude, 'It can never happen to me.' Such an attitude can lead to indifference. It is a recipe for inviting accidents and injuries. **Confidence leads to good output; overconfidence leads to bad outcome**.

5. **Being disorganised and unplanned:** Not thinking through a process can create major challenges. Starting something in haste without proper planning could lead to disaster. Hence, effective planning is a smart way to safety.

6. **Not taking pride in performance:** Pride in performance results in good performance and safety. It avoids all kinds of hazards. It sets standards for a good environment.

7. **Looking for short-term gain at the cost of long-term pain:** Everybody is looking to cut short on lead time or gestation, hence they look for shortcuts. **Shortcuts that reduce safety are classified as short-sightedness.** All of us like to work faster and more effectively. But shouldn't we ask that in the process of saving time, are we compromising on safety? If we don't ask this important question, we may be increasing the chances of casualties.

When we reach to pluck a rose in a clumsy manner, then we cannot complain about the thorns that prick our hands. **When there is carelessness, an accident is not a coincidence.**

Arrogance Leads to Casualty One of the greatest tragedies that took place out of sheer arrogance and casual attitude was the sinking of the unsinkable ship, Titanic. It happened in 1912. Titanic was at that time the world's largest ship weighing 46,328 tonnes, 882 feet long carrying almost 2,500 passengers. It was equipped with all the luxuries including a pool, gymnasium, mini-golf course, lavish dining rooms, etc. The Titanic struck an iceberg in the middle of the night ripping a hole through five of its sixteen water-tight compartments. It sank in a couple of hours killing 1,513 people.

The most unfortunate part of this tragedy was that the crew and the captain were warned that they were heading into ice fields. They were warned time after time, but they totally ignored all warnings, completely preoccupied with petty things. The Titanic brushed off the warning rather arrogantly by saying, '*Shut up, you are jamming my signals.*' Could this tragedy have been avoided? A hindsight answer is, yes.

The Titanic crew not only disregarded the warning, but also did not carry enough lifeboats and the unthinkable happened. The sinking of the Titanic was the price paid for arrogance and a casual attitude.

What a sad example of casual attitude leading to casualty.

If You Want To Achieve More, Don't Let Casual Attitude Leads To Casualties.

ACTION PLAN

- Write down three incidents that because of your casual attitude were detrimental to your life:

    i. _____

    ii. _____

    iii. _____

- How can you improve a casual attitude?

    i. _____

    ii. _____

    iii. _____

It's A Moral Obligation
For Every Honorable
Person To Be Prosperous
Because Money In
Good Hands Does Good
And Money In Evil Hands
Does Evil

CHAPTER 16 ——————————————————————

Become Prosperity Conscious

It would be a fair statement to say that every human being's ultimate aim in life is to be happy. Happiness can only be achieved if we have the following three things:

1. **Health**
2. **Wealth**
3. **Good Relationships**

In this chapter, we are going to cover **Wealth.** To lead a happy and fulfilling life, one of the most important ingredients needed is wealth. Wealth is not seen only in terms of a bank balance. It is physical wealth and relationship wealth put together. Wealth corresponds to **Financial Health** and **Financial Independence**. It is difficult to have spiritual, emotional and physical health without financial health.

Every society is divided into three groups of people — **Prosperous, Poor and Mediocre**. The poor and the prosperous can also be divided further into **super poor** and **super prosperous**.

Each group has a different mindset around money and goals. Our mindset and belief system have a lot to do with the physical manifestation of wealth. Each group gets exactly what it thinks about. An old saying, 'Seek and you shall find', holds true in our physical lives.

The goal for 'freedom' is primarily driven by the 'abundance mindset'. The goal for 'survival' and 'comfort' is primarily driven by a 'scarcity mindset'. With a 'scarcity mindset', one can only seek survival and comfort and nothing more.

• An article published in *Cleveland.com* on 14 January 2016 said, '"About 70 percent of people who win a lottery or get a big windfall actually end up broke in a few years", according to the National Endowment for Financial Education.'[1]

They had a windfall but mentally, for whatever reasons, they could not accept that they were millionaires. People with a scarcity mindset cannot hold their money. They imprudently invest or spend it, or it just gets squandered, wasted or lost.

It is well said that if you took the entire wealth of the world and distributed it equally among all people — in less than two years, it will probably come back into the same pockets again. Obviously, it's something to do with mindset.

---

[1] *http://www.cleveland.com/business/index.ssf/2016/01/why_do_70_percent_of_lottery_w.html*

Poverty Mindset There was once a beggar who would sit right in the middle of a busy street with a signboard that read, 'I'm a destitute, please help.' He would beg religiously. A young marketing executive used to pass by the beggar every day and occasionally drop some money into his bowl. One day, feeling pity, he asked the beggar how much money he made every day. The beggar said, *'Close to about $35.'* It occurred to him to change the signboard to something more compelling for the passer-by to donate. He created a new placard for the beggar that read, 'In case you have charity on your mind once a month, why not do it here?'

The signboard worked. People stopped to read and started donating. Within three hours, the beggar collected close to about $50 and interestingly, wrapped up, packed up and was gone.

Had he stayed there for the whole day, he might have been able to collect close to a $100. Who knows? Mentally, he had set up his own limit. He had conditioned himself to collect only so much and no more.

Let me narrate to you a real life story. In the mid-1970s, the president of Uganda, Idi Amin had ordered the expulsion of his country's Asian people. These people, who were settled there for generations, became refugees overnight and fled the country, leaving all their assets behind. A few thousand took refuge as migrants in Canada. All of them literally started from ground zero. Interestingly, here's what I observed.

Those who were doing well in Uganda were the same people who started doing well in Canada as well. They worked hard. They were putting in long hours—twelve to fourteen hours a day was a common practice. Some of them who started working at shops eventually ended up buying those very shops. I noticed that these people not only became financially stable, but also helped others to grow. Similarly, those who were moaners and groaners in Uganda were also the moaners and groaners in Canada too. People who started doing well in Canada, despite obstacles, had a mindset to go beyond survival to become financially independent and then they did. The above example clearly establishes a relationship between mindset and prosperity.

It's all about the mindset!

Prosperity Conscious, Poverty Conscious and Mediocre

1. Prosperity Conscious

The prosperity conscious have a mindset to seek freedom. The prosperous always think of abundance. They think that the universe provides 'in abundance' for everyone. **Prosperity consciousness is a state of mind**. By bearing the 'prosperity mindset', one can attract financial well-being and live a happy life. Those who seek freedom end up achieving financial health and much more.

2. Poverty Conscious

Those who are poverty conscious have a mindset that seeks only survival. They are the ones who have a sea of opportunities, but choose not to go out to achieve them. **Poverty consciousness is a state of mind.** By bearing the 'poverty mindset', one can never attract financial health, and continues to live a sad life. Such people believe that there is scarcity of things or there is not enough.

3. Mediocre

The mediocre have a mindset to seek comfort. The mediocre think only of comfort. They are ones who do not want to strive too high nor do they want to be left out. However, the word mediocre has negative undertones. It implies that the person is average with moderate abilities and that he is incapable of achieving more than what he actually does.

Prosperity Conscious Busy Themselves in Attaining Financial Independence

The prosperity conscious choose their advisors very carefully. They are willing to pay for good advice. It is not unusual that, many times, the free advice ends up being the most expensive one. Free advice by and large is not expert guidance. Generally, it is given by those who give their opinions without any knowledge or experience. Prosperity conscious people choose to take advice from those who have done something worthwhile not from 'living failures'.

Prosperity conscious people seek **freedom**, which is achieved through financial independence.

They realise that consistency and self-discipline go hand-in-hand resulting in freedom.

Let's look at what financial independence is.

Financial Independence

We need to qualify the term **Financial Independence**. Financial independence to some means, **'having enough financial reserve for contingencies and retirement'**. This is called a 'nest egg', but it is not financial independence. Financial independence is **'creating a big enough net-worth that generates enough passive income that allows us the freedom to do what we want to do, or work because we want to work not because we have to'**. This is called creating a goose that lays 'golden eggs' and that's what prosperity conscious people work towards.

Pretty much all over the world, people start working between the ages of 20–25 and retire at 65; but interestingly, in the US, only 5 per cent of them are considered to be financially independent. After 40–45 years of working lives, 95 per cent people have nothing to show, they are either dead or dead broke. They are either dependent on friends, relatives or social security, or are still working. Only 5 per cent are financially independent. The statistics are alarming for a country that is considered the land of opportunities. Here is a country where everybody has an equal opportunity and the potential to be a millionaire and yet most people don't recognise, neglect or let pass these opportunities. How sad! The question is do we want to fall into the 95 per cent or the 5 per cent?

It was estimated that in the year 1950, there were only 100,000 millionaires.

And, according to *businessinsider.in*, dated 14 November 2017, 'Since 2016, there are 36 million millionaires in the world.' The rate of growth of millionaires every year is exponential.

Shouldn't we also be part of the success story of becoming financially independent? Our objective in life should be freedom through financial independence.

By and large, people who are astute with money, put it into the following four pockets:

1. **Investment**
2. **Savings**
3. **Spending**
4. **Donation**

All monetary receipts in life should go into these four slots of the 'piggy bank of life'.

Out of the total money that we receive periodically, how much should go into which slot is the real question.

The first 10–15 per cent of the total money should go into **investment**. Out of the balance, the next 10 per cent should go into **savings** and emergency fund (a minimum of six months to one year worth of income should be kept as liquid savings), and then whatever is left should be divided between **spending** and

donation, simultaneously. Obviously, here I am not talking of the abject poor, who have nothing left after survival.

Investing money is for long-term growth.

Saving money is to meet short-term emergencies.

Spending money is for sustenance.

Donation is the philanthropic aspect of serving society.

The four pockets of the piggy bank can further be condensed into two pockets.

When money comes, either:

1. We invest it, or
2. We spend it (waste)

What we invest gives us a return, but what we spend is lost forever.

Warren Buffet said, '**Do not save what is left after spending, but spend what is left after saving.**'

> *Prosperity conscious people save first and spend what is left after saving, while the poverty conscious do the reverse.*

Prosperity Conscious People Create Assets

What's an asset? An asset is defined as an investment that generates a passive income. Passive income is money that is automatically generated: it is like a perpetual inflow without your active involvement of skill, labour and time. You ask anybody, by and large, people will say a house is an asset. It is an asset if it's generating a rental income, not otherwise. Think about this. If you're living in a house, is it giving you any income? If the answer is no, then it is not an asset. It's a liability. There are upkeep and taxes—you're putting money out of your pocket. It is a part of your wealth, but not your asset in this case. It could be a part of your net-worth upon liquidation though. We should look at creating 'Real Assets'. **If you have savings, always buy a second home rather than a second car** as the first home could be your residence and the second one could generate an income. In such a case, the second home automatically becomes your real asset.

Besides, the value of the house could appreciate, whereas the value of the car, invariably, depreciates.

Prosperity Conscious Conserve Their Resources

Prosperity conscious people know the value of the fortune they earn. They believe in conserving their resources and saving rather than carelessly spending their fortune. They live humble lives, because they live for self-satisfaction and not for public screening. It is a misconception that millionaires and multi-millionaires are pretentiously flashy and they only buy designer stuff—shirts worth $3,000-4,000, Rolex watches, drive expensive Mercedes and BMWs, or always travel first class.

The American businessman and philanthropist, Warren Buffet, perpetually ranked among the world's richest men, lives a lifestyle that hasn't changed much since before he became prosperous. He continues to live in the same house in the central Dundee neighborhood of Omaha that he bought in 1958 for $31,500 and his tastes are as humble as before.

Infosys's co-founder, Narayana Murthy, a billionaire, still lives in a middle-class home and travels economy class. His only known indulgence is books.

Prosperity conscious people are culturally and financially rich, but they were already culturally rich before they became financially rich. Being culturally rich is the major distinguishing factor between the prosperity conscious and the poverty conscious.

The *nouveau riche* (new rich), on the other hand, have gained financial wealth, but lack 'cultural wealth'. Hence, through their ostentatious behaviour, they announce to the whole world that they have arrived. They always look to gain attention. They look to get acceptance from the world, because they lack self-acceptance. They are envious of what others have and they resent other people's successes.

They don't understand the truth of life — **that people make things, things don't make people**. They lack the basic understanding of the difference between net-worth and self-worth. **They measure self-worth based on net-worth**.

For many people earning a fortune may seem to be difficult, but so would it be to comprehend the basic and humble lifestyle of these self-made millionaires. Remember, **material happiness is temporary—it doesn't last forever.**

Prosperity Conscious are Far-Sighted

The poor and the mediocre basically think from month-to-month, such as taking care of their living expenses, mortgages, credit cards, etc., whereas the prosperity conscious are far-sighted. They think and plan in terms of decades. They prepare accordingly. They think in terms of financial literacy, investments, how to save taxes legally and how to make their money work for them.

Profits and Wages

Prosperity conscious people understand the difference between profits and wages. They look to get paid for results, whereas poverty conscious people look to get paid for their time. Prosperity conscious people look for profits, poverty conscious people look for wages. Prosperity conscious have self-interest in mind but not selfishness.

> **Self-interest says:** *For me to win, the world does not have to lose — we can win-win together.*
>
> **Selfishness says:** *For me to win, I don't care if the world loses.*

Prosperity conscious people understand the difference between active income and passive income. They learn and plan to pass their assets from one generation to the next. The more a person thinks into the future, the more prosperous he is likely to become in life. The prosperous ask themselves — how can we:

1. Multiply our income and legally reduce our taxes?
2. Where would we be 10 years from now?

*   According to *Stanford.edu*, 2007, Mr Warren Buffett said, 'That he was taxed at 17.7 per cent on the $46 million he made last year, without trying to avoid paying higher taxes, while his secretary, who earned $60,000, was taxed at 30 per cent.'[2]

> *People with poor and mediocre mindsets always think of instant gratification.*

People with poor and mediocre mindsets will do anything to satisfy their impulses. They will not hesitate to take a loan, debt or charge on credit card, whether or not they can afford it. Their urge to get gratification instantly is greater than their good sense. Whereas, far-sighted people would not mind delaying gratification because their ultimate goal is freedom and not survival or comfort. Prosperity conscious people develop and live by the discipline of delayed gratification.

---

[2] *http://tusb.stanford.edu/2007/07/warren_buffet_has_a_lower_tax.html*

> *Forgo little pleasures today and enjoy big tomorrow, or enjoy big today and forgo big pleasures tomorrow.*

The poor and the mediocre put their lives in the charge of others, which by default turn out to be the prosperity conscious. Prosperity conscious people prefer freedom over comfort, whereas mediocre prefer comfort over freedom, hence, they stay limited to comfort and never achieve freedom.

This principle of far-sighted thinking not only applies to our financial position, but to every area of life. **Prosperity conscious people apply far-sighted thinking in every area of their lives even to developing strong relationships and sound health.** Isn't the same thing true in our relationships with others? When we think long-term, would we not think of giving more respect to others and having better relationships? Wouldn't we think of win-win relationships? Short-term thinking only makes us look for 'what's in it for me', 'what can I get from them', or 'what others can do for me.' Such thinking only ends up in using other people as tools for personal gain. **Those who use other people only for their own selfish gains end up as very lonely people in life.**

Prosperity conscious people always develop long-term relationships with no ulterior motive, but which naturally results in financial success. This is nature's law. Whether it is family, friends, customers, or anybody for that matter, they always think of how best they can benefit and serve others.

How do we measure true wealth? It is not by our bank balance, but in the relationships that we build. This is what makes us emotionally strong — indeed is our true wealth. **If you have a billion dollars, but are emotionally bankrupt, then you are the poorest person on this earth**. Just the way there is financial poverty, emotional poverty is real among people. People who carry hatred, greed, impatience and lack empathy are very poor emotionally. Strong relationships are very fulfilling and make people secure in life. Prosperity conscious people always think long-term in their physical, financial, and emotional life.

Is it not wise to think long-term about physical health? If the answer is yes, then a person will make time to exercise and eat healthy food regularly, whereas if you think only of short-term gratification, then you will not mind neglecting exercise and eating junk food resulting in weight gain and low energy levels. Far-sighted thinking empowers a person with energy to become financially prosperous.

Secrets of the far-sighted and potentially prosperous:

1. They make their passion their vocation.
2. They do what they love to do and end up earning money.
3. They strive to make themselves prosperous in all areas of their lives — physically, financially, mentally, emotionally and spiritually.

If a person wants to move from a poor or mediocre

state to a prosperous state, they must plan their lives with farsighted thinking.

Long-term goals help you develop perseverance. All prosperous people have faced setbacks and challenges in life, but through preseverance have bounced back. The mediocre and the poor give up the moment, the going gets tough. Prosperous people go through setbacks one after the other but they persevere. They do whatever it takes to achieve success and freedom, ethically.

Instant Gratification The Western world, especially the US, is suffering from a financial crisis because of instant gratification. Instant gratification says, 'I want it and I want it now', whether I can afford it or not.

We pay with credit cards even when it is beyond our means. Even the governments of many countries are spending beyond their means. **We keep buying things that we don't need with the money that we don't have trying to impress the people we don't like.**

Achievers Do Today What Others Don't So They Can Enjoy Things Tomorrow, Which Others Won't. They Love To Be In Charge Of Their Lives.

ACTION PLAN

- What kind of a mindset do you most resonate with?

- What three actions would you take to become prosperity conscious?

    i. _____

    ii. _____

    iii. _____

- Write down three things you would do differently in order to structure your finances to become prosperity conscious:

    i. _____

    ii. _____

    iii. _____

CHAPTER 17 ─────────────────

Fire Within

Wise Thinking, Courageous Action

Courage is the faith one has in oneself to outperform fear. Faith gives strength but doubts lead to weakness. Courage is strength in the face of pain and grief. It is not absence of fear, but the conquest of fear. Courageous people face trying situations with wisdom to preserve honour, whereas cowards are inclined to take the easy path.

There is a story from ancient times about a mean moneylender, who had lent money to a trader. Because of setbacks, one after the other, the trader was unable to pay back his debt. The trader had a pretty, young daughter and the devious moneylender had his eye on her. Pretending to be helpful, he suggested that if the trader would agree to him marrying his young girl, he would forgive the debt. Otherwise, if he did not pay, all hell would break loose. Both the trader and the daughter were in a fix. The moneylender, pretending to be generous, proposed an idea and said that they should let fate decide. He proposed that he would put one black pebble and one white pebble into an empty bag and the girl should pick one pebble. If she picked the black pebble, she would have to marry him and the father's debt would be forgiven; but if she picked the white pebble, she would not have to marry him and the debt would still be forgiven. The daughter was not just pretty, but also very intelligent. She didn't want her father to go to jail so she agreed to the proposition. The day came when the whole village came to see the fate of the trader and his daughter. They were standing on the bank of the river that was full of pebbles. The moneylender stooped down to pick up the two pebbles. Making sure nobody was noticing, he picked two black pebbles so that he could make sure he married the girl. Quietly, the girl was watching. The girl was then asked to pick one pebble upon which her and her father's fate rested.

Supposing we were among the spectators while this was happening:

1. What would we have done?
2. What would we have advised the girl to do?
3. How would we have handled the situation?
4. What choices did the girl have?

    i. She could expose the moneylender by asking him to show both the pebbles.
    ii. She could refuse and sacrifice her father.
    iii. She could take a black pebble and sacrifice herself to save her father.

The choices were not easy. It was either her life or

her father's life at stake, and she was not prepared to sacrifice either, especially father's.

Here is what the girl did:

She put her hand in the bag and picked one pebble knowing fully well that they were both black. She was the only one who had seen what the moneylender had done. As she pulled her hand out of the bag, without looking at the pebble, she purposely lost her balance, fell on the ground, and dropped the pebble. It got mixed up with the others so nobody could see what colour it was. She got up, apologised for her clumsiness and said, *'Let's check what colour pebble is in the bag – that will tell us which one I picked.'* The pebble in the bag was of course black, and it was assumed that the one she had picked was white. In front of the whole village, the moneylender did not have the guts to accept his dishonesty. He had to live with his decision and both the father and the daughter went free. Her action was guided by the motivation to preserve honour. It was her courage that helped her maintain her cool and think of a creative solution. Her quick thinking showed that **wisdom is nothing more than the timely application of creativity and common sense.** Only courageous people accept the challenges of life so that they can live with respect and dignity.

Men of principles are bold but not all bold people are men of principles.

We often do things either to gain pleasure or to avoid pain. Morally, cowards do not have the courage to pay the price to defend their beliefs. Courage lies not in accepting conditions blindly, but in daring to face the consequences. The ability to believe in ourselves when everyone has given up on us is a sign of courage. We know that we are vulnerable, and yet we endure. **Our faith in ourselves helps turn dreams into reality**. A great example in history is that of Galileo.

Galileo Stood His Ground At the age of twenty-six, Galileo became a professor of Mathematics at the University of Pisa. At that time people accepted all the ancient theories without questioning them. The ancient Greek philosopher, Aristotle, was considered the greatest of all authorities. Questioning his theories was considered disrespectful. Galileo proved that the weight of an object has nothing to do with how fast the object falls. The rate of descent of an object depends on the resistance of air. This went against Aristotle's theory. Even though Galileo was able to demonstrate his theory, people chose not to believe him. They were afraid that discrediting one of Aristotle's principles may lead to proving his other principles wrong too, and this made them feel threatened. No one came forward in support of Galileo but the great scientist did not lose faith in himself. He stood his ground, and in time, his theory met with both approval and acclaim.

Courage is Neither Fearlessness Nor Reckless Behaviour

Courage is confronting and conquering fear. Recklessness often grows out of naievity, vanity and/or foolishness. The ability to choose the correct action requires wisdom. **Courage is a demonstration of the wisdom to know when to take a firm stand.** Recklessness, on the other hand, can embarrass and even endanger people. It can lead to loss of trust. Courageous behaviour inspires people and helps generate trust.

The courage displayed by Martin Luther King Jr. and Nelson Mandela inspired others to stand against injustice even at the cost of great personal hardships. The movements they led achieved much for their followers, their countries, and society at large.

Courage is a State of Mind

Strength and authority demonstrated by bullying or oppressing the innocent is not courage but cowardice. Bullying and oppression are a cover-up for insecurity. Courage is a state of mind. It can be cultivated but never faked. It is not a onetime act but an automatic response. Courage empowers us to face life squarely, move forward, and take charge.

Courage is the most important value which makes all other values possible. The courage and ability to take decisions puts a person in the driver's seat. If we do not take control of our future, our future is automatically determined by other people's decisions. We have to move forward with the belief that our actions are worthwhile, only then, courage comes easier.

Human beings who lack courage are a sad spectacle. People feel inadequate and lose their self-respect when they do not find the courage to respond to situations in life.

John McEnroe said, '*I was pleased with the 1988 Wimbledon because I pushed myself. At one point, I started getting a cramp in my foot, then my knee hurt. But I pushed myself anyway. I felt that I did my best. It was like, I was playing from within.*'

PLAYERS PREPARE, PLAYERS WIN, PLAYERS LOSE; but PLAYERS PLAY, and they PLAY FAIR. Courage enables a person to face hardships without giving into fear.

> *Neutrality on issues of integrity amounts to cowardice.*

Test of Courage — After years of hard work, Thomas Carlyle finished the manuscript of his book, *The French Revolution*, and gave it to a friend to read. The friend's housekeeper mistook the manuscript for trash and threw it into the fire. When Carlyle's wife got the news, she could not hold back her tears. His friend stood trembling, and Carlyle himself was speechless. Finally, with a display of remarkable courage and restraint he said, '*Accidents like these happen.*' Although, outwardly,

Carlyle appeared courageous, he was devastated. He was unsure if he could continue with the project. He could not sleep all night.

The next morning he resolved to start working on his book again. No matter what, he just could not give up. Two years later, he had recreated and finished his great work, *The French Revolution*, which remains to this day a living testimony to his undefeatable spirit.

The greatest test of courage is accepting loss without losing heart. Challenges in life make or break us depending on the stuff we are made up of and the goals we want to achieve in life. The important thing is to know how to rise above the innumerable disappointments that life has in store for most of us and achieve our goals inspite of these disappointments.

The Sweet Music of Applause As a child, Ludwig Beethoven could play the piano better than most adults. His father, a drunkard, was more interested in the money he could make using his son, but his mother was supportive. Ludwig was seventeen when she died, leaving two younger brothers under his care. Young Beethoven soon grew to be recognised as a truly great musician; but misfortune struck when at the age of twenty-eight he became deaf. Deafness for a musician is especially cruel. But Beethoven overcame his disability with great courage and wrote some of his best music after he had lost his ability to hear. At one time, Beethoven agreed to conduct an orchestra at Vienna. With his back towards the audience, he directed the music that he himself could not hear. The audience was enthralled. When the recital was over, he kept standing with his back towards the audience, getting his things together and packing up to leave. One of his companions understood what was happening and turned him around. Only then did Beethoven see that he was receiving a standing ovation. The audience, who saw that Beethoven could neither hear his own composition nor their standing ovation, was moved to tears by his exemplary courage. **Overcoming adversity takes exceptional inner strength,** was beautifully demonstrated by Beethoven.

Courage to Care   Marquis de Lafayette, a brave soldier of the American Revolution returned to his estate in France in 1782. He was a man known for his courage, integrity, and idealism both in the US and France. In 1783, though the wheat harvests in France were poor, Lafayette's barns were full. The foreman of his estate advised that he should sell the wheat as prices were sky-rocketing. To this Lafayette, knowing that the peasants of the surrounding villages were hungry, responded, 'No, this is the time to give.' This is demonstration of moral courage. Caring comes from empathy. To a caring person, the honour of the other person is just as important as his own. An honourable person does not put a price tag on humanity. To them, dignity is more important than financial gains.

Every act of love and care involves giving, and hence, is an act of courage. To act courageously requires soul-searching and intelligence. Courageous action may not always bring happiness, but there is no happiness without courageous action.

Courage to Dare

By the age of twenty-one, Copernicus was a learned man with extraordinary abilities. Popular belief at that time held that the earth was the centre of the universe and that the sun and the stars moved around it. The influential men then were the priests and the astrologers who gave their own interpretation of the heavens. Copernicus had the wisdom to see through the ignorance of the astrologers. He conducted his own study and found that the earth was not the centre of the universe, but a small planet that revolved around the sun. His discoveries were not in tune with the times. Thus, he faced resistance from the Vatican, and the priests publicly denounced him. He was exiled and forbidden by the Church from speaking publicly on any matter that threatened the common belief as expounded by the Church. Secretly, some people respected him and his work, but felt unsure about his sanity. Undaunted, Copernicus carried on writing about his newfound knowledge and after decades of effort, he completed his work. Now, the insurmountable problem ahead of him was to get his findings published. Ever persistent, he went ahead and dedicated his book to Pope Paul III, a scholar, knowing fully well that only the Pope would be capable of handling any opposition arising from the publication of his controversial book. In 1543, when Copernicus was on his deathbed, a messenger came and handed him a copy of his published book. Holding the book to his heart, he breathed his last. Copernicus' courage and strength of conviction paid him rich dividends.

> **Popular beliefs may not always be right. They sometimes need to be challenged against all odds.**

- In 1914, Thomas Edison's factory in West Orange, New Jersey, caught fire. He was sixty-seven years old then. Although the damage exceeded $2 million, the buildings were insured for only $238,000. Looking at the factory go up in flames, Edison stood calmly and watched. He saw his son and said, *'Call your mother. Bring her here. She will never see anything like this as long as she lives.'*

  The next morning, Edison looked at the ruins and said, *'There is great value in disaster. All our mistakes are burned up. Thank God we can start anew[1].'*

What an attitude! It takes tremendous guts and courage to face a situation like this.

Courage Multiplies Our Abilities

Whenever two people of an equal ability compete, it is the more courageous of the two

---

[1] *https://www.linkedin.com/pulse/thomas-edison-great-value-disaster-all-our-mistakes-gone-attaway*

who wins. The courage we display can make the opponent wary and put him on the defensive.

> *One individual with a backbone will accomplish more than a hundred men with a wishbone.*

Courage is that firmness which confronts danger. It requires taking risks and seeking the unknown with a sense of responsibility towards oneself and those around them.

Louis Braille was born in France about 200 years ago. His father made leather goods. One day, he hurt his eye while playing with an instrument used for stitching leather. The infection spread to the other eye and he became totally blind. Blind people those days were treated with great cruelty, and their affliction was often seen as divine punishment. Louis' father sent him to a blind school where he met a retired soldier who taught him to read with the help of embossed dots. Braille started refining the script for the blind so that they could read by feeling with their fingers. By the age of twenty, Braille had conceived and published a book explaining how his system could be used by the blind for reading and writing. Braille not only overcame his own affliction but also helped blind people all over the world to empower themselves by reading and acquiring knowledge. Braille's method soon spread across the world. His story is an example of true courage in the face of the most trying circumstances!

People like Braille have enriched the world and will be honoured till eternity.

Five Steps to Develop Courage More important than what we get in life is what we become. Life is precious and priceless, and so are we. When we change ourselves, we also change the world around us. 'What we do' and 'what we are' are inextricably linked in a dynamic cycle. As rational beings we can consciously change our thinking pattern and behaviour. The steps outlined below help us develop courage:

1. Face Up to Reality

When we don't have the courage to face up to the situation, we look for an escape route which is called rationalisation. Rationalisation is a psychological defence commonly used to avoid dealing with painful realities. Refusing to acknowledge and accept reality becomes a mindset. When we don't accept reality we start living either in the past or in the future. We don't stop there. We distort reality and build up fears and doubts. We worry about things that may never happen. Such imagined fears weaken a person. We need to face up to reality and stop rationalising.

2. Take a Stand

Re-examine your value-system. Guidance may be sought from people who have a clear value system and the courage to take a stand.

3. Build Character

Character is the foundation that helps us confront our false beliefs and build moral courage. We need to review our core values and principles to build character.

4. Practise Little Acts of Courage

Every little act of courage makes us more courageous to face bigger challenges. Courage is not like money in the bank. In fact, the more we spend it the more we get in return. We often avoid acting courageously out of reasons like complacence and apathy. We then become so comfortable with our discomfort that we start loving it. The trouble is that many of the problems we face today may have been solved more easily with a small courageous decision taken at the right time.

5. Perfect Practise Leads to Preparation

Prepare by trying to anticipate situations, and then be ready for the totally unexpected. Remember, practice does not make us perfect, but makes permanent whatever we practise. Small choices in life end up becoming significant choices and prepare a person to face the bigger challenges of life.

To Achieve More Honourably, Takes Courage.

ACTION PLAN

- Write down three acts of courage that you've displayed and you're proud of.

    i. _____

    ii. _____

    iii. _____

- Let's check your courage quotient. Tick the option that best applies to the following questions:

    i. I hold myself back because of the fear of making mistakes
       a. Strongly Disagree   b. Disagree
       c. Neutral   d. Agree
       e. Strongly Agree

    ii. I'm afraid of changes
       a. Strongly Disagree   b. Disagree
       c. Neutral   d. Agree
       e. Strongly Agree

    iii. I take risks only if I know they would pay off
       a. Strongly Disagree   b. Disagree
       c. Neutral   d. Agree
       e. Strongly Agree

    iv. I will not mind getting into a conflict if it's for an overall good
       a. Strongly Disagree   b. Disagree
       c. Neutral   d. Agree
       e. Strongly Agree

    v. Intense pressure will not deter me from completing my responsibilities
       a. Strongly Disagree   b. Disagree

      c. Neutral   d. Agree

      e. Strongly Agree

iv. I like to take up challenging tasks.

      a. Strongly Disagree   b. Disagree

      c. Neutral   d. Agree

      e. Strongly Agree

Strongly disagree and disagree reflect a high courage quotient.

Agree and strongly agree shows you where you need to develop more courage.

• Think of three incidents where you did not practise courage but going forward, you will.

    i. _____

    ii. _____

    iii. _____

We Are
Accountable Not Only
For Our Actions,
But Also For Our
Inactions

——————————————

CHAPTER 18

Accountability

" *Every sunrise brings new opportunities and every sunset demands results and accountability.* **"**

Many times, we hear, 'People are our greatest assets.' This statement is not really true. **People are not assets, only 'good people' are assets, the rest are all liabilities.** Goodness always needs to be cultivated, evil happens. If we want to have a good garden we must consciously plant seeds of good flowers and fruits. Weeds keep coming automatically, but cultivating goodness takes hard work and conscious effort.

I Can Sleep When the Wind Blows   Once upon a time, there was a farmer who desperately needed a working hand at his farm. Good help was hard to find. He had hired and fired many people. Eventually, he interviewed one and asked, *'What can you do at the farm?'* The man very confidently replied, '*I can sleep when the wind blows.*' The farmer did not understand what it meant, but out of desperation hired the man. Every day the man did his job well. One night, it seemed like a major storm was coming. The farmer got concerned about his harvested crop and cattle. As the storm got worse, he quickly ran to his help, who was sleeping, woke him up, and said, '*Get up quickly and let's prepare to handle the crops and shelter the animals.*' The help said, '*There is no need to get up. I am sleeping and you can also go to sleep.*' Hearing this kind of a callous and non-caring answer the farmer got very angry. Time was running short and he ran outside to take care of things. What he saw stunned him—the grain was all well covered with tarpaulin and the animals were all protected in the barn. He had to do nothing. He went back into his home to relax and sleep. Now he could understand the true meaning of what his help said when he was hired, '*I can sleep when the wind blows.*'

What is the moral of the story? The moral is that the person who was hired was a good person, he was an asset and not a liability, someone who owned his responsibilities well—he knew he 'could sleep when the wind blows', because he would have taken care of the situation 'before the wind blows'. His preparedness became an asset for the farmer. The above story is literally a lesson for life. It's a philosophy to live by.

Accountability is a Way of Life

Those who accept accountability take pride in performance. People who take pride in performance anticipate what's coming next. They don't wait for the need or problem to arise, they preempt and prevent probable mishaps by taking preventive actions. They are prepared in advance to resolve the problems or meet the needs before they arise. People who mean business always have a contingency plan. **They perform and deliver no matter what. They deliver results not excuses.**

Recently, I shared the dais with the chairperson of a five-star hotel, who is considered to be the pioneer in providing one of the best hospitality services in the industry, globally. I asked him how he was able to provide such great service consistently. He said, *'There is no secret. Our entire training of service is based on the philosophy of the anticipation of customer's needs.'* He further said, *'Many of our hotels are in tropical countries where the weather gets pretty hot. When a customer walks in from the burning heat outside, we anticipate that he would need a refreshing cold towel and a cold drink, and we offer them that even before they ask for it. This example is just a fragment of the philosophy the hotel's concept of service is based upon. At every touch point, the philosophy of the anticipation of the customer's need prevails.'*

They believe in the philosophy — it is better to **PREPARE AND PREVENT** than to **REPAIR AND REPENT.**

Accountability is defined as willingness to accept responsibility: When we accept accountability willingly, it automatically becomes an obligation. The word willingly means, 'I accept out of choice and not out of duress or pressure.' They are all positive words that prevent negative consequences. None of them are corrective words. People deal with us based on their perception of our commitment to what we say. Only a person who holds himself accountable will work towards keeping commitments. We always need to ask ourselves the following questions:

1. Am I trustworthy?
2. Am I reliable?
3. Can people accept my word?
4. Can people depend on me?

Only if the answer to these questions is—yes, can we be termed as accountable.

Average people look for above average incomes. What they really need to be asked is:

- Are you an above average person?
- Do you have above average enthusiasm?
- Do you have above average relationships?
- Do you have above average health?
- Do you have above average passion?
- Do you have above average humour?
- Do you have above average integrity?
- Do you put in above average hard work?

Think about it. Are you that person?

How can you get anything above average in life when you are only 'average'?

We need to become above average before we can get anything above average.

Average is Not Good Enough The world doesn't reward 'average'.

- When you go out dining, do you look for an average restaurant?
- When you want to be served, do you look for an average waiter?
- When you look for a sumptuous meal, do you look for average food?
- When you fall sick, do you look for an average doctor?
- When you need advice, do you look for an average consultant?
- When you want to get married, do you look for an average life-partner?

Average is defined as, **'Lowest of the best and highest of the worst'.** It simply means that if I have one leg in fire and the other in ice, on an average I should be fine and comfortable. Average is not good enough.

- According to an article, '*99.9 per cent may not be good enough*', 'A defect or wacky loss scenario may occur only 1 per cent of the time, or even only 0.1 per cent. A standard of 99.9 per cent effectiveness sounds impressive and — in very few contexts — it may be, but consider that if 99.9 per cent was good enough, then in US…

If 99.9 Per cent were Good Enough, then...

- 22,000 checks will be deducted from the wrong bank accounts in the next sixty minutes
- 1,314 phone calls will be misplaced by telecommunication services every minute.
- 2,488,200 books will be shipped in the next twelve months with the wrong cover.

- Two plane landings daily at O'Hare International Airport in Chicago will be unsafe.
- 18,322 pieces of mail will be mishandled in the next hour.
- 291 pacemaker operations will be performed incorrectly this year.
- 12 babies will be given to the wrong parents each day.[1]

Even though 99.9 per cent is not average, it is still not good enough, so how can average be good enough?

Before we can ever have anything in life, we must become someone with a sense of ownership, integrity, and accountability.

Lack of personal accountability has become an epidemic problem. Finger pointing and blaming others is the typical behavioural pattern of failures.

Imagine that in a restaurant you are served a dish different from the one you ordered. You ask the waiter how this mess happened. He replies, 'Oops, people in the kitchen goofed up.' Rather than accepting responsibility, he put the blame on somebody else. Such people raise very important questions:

1. Why did he bring the wrong dish?
2. Why did he not check the order before serving?
3. When will they learn?
4. Why can't we find responsible people?

All these questions demonstrate a severe dearth of people who practise personal responsibility and

---

[1] *http://milestoneconsultingincmotivation.blogspot.in/2013/04/if-999-were-good-enough.html*

accountability. People who accept accountability, live better, more satisfying and enjoyable lives.

Accepting personal accountability solves problems and leads to astonishing results. Just like a poor sailor blames the wind, similarly people who don't accept accountability make excuses and give justifications.

Power of Accountability Whenever someone says to us, 'I shall hold you accountable', what is the first thought that comes to our minds? Is it fear or a feeling of being threatened? Do people then look for a scapegoat because of non-performance? Is there a feeling of pressure or stress? Most people associate the word accountability with consequences or punishment for not meeting expectations.

In fact, it is quite the opposite. The reality is that there is no success without accountability. **Accountability is a prerequisite to success.** Good leaders and organisations establish accountability upfront. **Accountability is the foundation to better relationships — it avoids unpleasant surprises and eventually leads to positive outcomes.**

Look at two scenarios to understand the power of accountability:

1. The accountant told the President that the final accounting would be completed by 15 April before 5.00 pm. Two of the senior colleagues asked the President, '*Do you trust the accountant fully? Are you going to hold him accountable?*' The

President replied, *'I know him well. He always keeps his word.'*

The accountant's accountability won him the President's trust.

2. Suppose we had asked one of our executives to send a report to a client by 11.00 pm. We get a call from the client saying, *'The report was due at 11:00 pm. It's 1:00 am now. How come I haven't received it yet? When can I expect it?'* Now, due to the urgent nature of the matter, this odd timing had to be adhered to. What happens here? We lose face and our credibility. We ask the executive the reason for the delay and he says, *'I got stuck in some personal work. I am sending it.'*

Unless there was an emergency, should he have indulged in personal work? This is totally irresponsible behaviour. In case there was an emergency, should he not have informed the client of the delay? Informing the client is not a favour, it's an obligation.

His irresponsibility made the organisation lose credibility. We paid a price as we lost face in front of the client. And the executive paid a price as he lost our trust in him. Bottom line is — this could even lead to a loss of future business.

Where accountability is involved, seniors and juniors are equally accountable to one another. The objective of accountability is to help each other perform at a higher level and succeed, rather than pull each other down.

Red Alert A dangerous sign would be when we mess up and nobody says anything, nobody holds us accountable for our mistake. This would simply mean that everyone has stopped relying and given up on us. They feel we are not worth wasting their time on. To have a high-performance culture, one needs to drive accountability into one's organisation. In order to manage performance and accountability, we need to ask:

1. Knowing what they know now, would they hire us again?
2. Are we or am I the best person for the job?

Accountability is only a reflection of culture.

The following are effective ways to teach accountability to our teams:

1. **Holding people accountable**. Do not be afraid to ask for an explanation. Ask them when will they keep their commitment. Look into their eyes and ask them, *'You said you would, but you didn't. When are you going to do it?'* Don't be afraid to confront.
2. **Ask questions, without making it personal.** Tell them that we have nothing personal against them. Do not accept vague answers. Question their explanations. If you ask someone at office, *'How many times did you read the script?'* and his reply is, *'Around twenty times'*, then you need to be sure what is around twenty times. It can either be eighteen, nineteen or twenty. It's a number and it cannot be 'around'.
    Similarly, if you ask the executive, *'How many sales calls did you make last week?'* and he says, 'around

fifteen', then what does it mean? Did the person make eleven or twelve or thirteen or fourteen calls or maybe just one or two? Do not let them get away by being evasive.

3. **Be specific in our communication**. Stop making vague statements. Specific statements have the power to move people. 'What can I expect from you?' Be specific. What moves people are deadlines. Just like there are deadlines in sports, there are deadlines in business. There is a deadline to our existence as well. Minimise generalised statements.

4. **Make expectations clear and measurable**. Haven't we heard people say, '*I am working hard, but nothing is working out?*' This statement is mathematically wrong and factually false. It only makes logical sense that I have to improve. Numbers do not lie. Learn to make realistic expectations and stick to them.

5. **Establish consequences in case of failure.** Does that mean threatening to fire people? Can CEOs get fired? The answer is yes. Customers can fire them. The employees can fire them. The stockholders can fire them. Even vendors can fire them. Consequences of non-performance have to be borne by the CEO just as much as others.

6. **Coach our people.** Giving people the right skills is imperative. This can be done by:

    i. Teaching theoretically with explanations and examples
    ii. Demonstrating

   iii. Practically making them do it
   iv. Testing for understanding
    v. Repeating to reinforce
   vi. Practising to internalise

   The best way to coach your people is to become a role model for them. What they see, they learn.

7. **Close all conversations on a positive note**. Build their self-esteem and hold them accountable. A boosted self-esteem acts as encouragement to repeat positive behaviour.

How Does Accountability Work?

For accountability to be met, expectations and deliverables for both parties should be crystal clear. This needs good communication skills. One way to confirm understanding is to ask the other party to paraphrase what was said. In a situation like this, both parties are responsible: the giver and the receiver. For example — if the manager said, '*I expect you to perform well*', the expression 'perform well' is subjective. The receiver should ask the manager to quantify and elaborate. Otherwise, the communication remains incomplete. Now, when the manager quantifies, communication is complete.

Both parties need to understand the meaning of 'perform well'. Outcomes must be clear. For accountability to be sustained, measurable quality standards must be established. Organisations that have a culture of accountability make it a practice to only hire and retain employees who accept accountability as a personal value.

The following are advantages of accountability:

1. It increases your level of performance.
2. It helps avoid unpleasant surprises.
3. It gives greater job satisfaction.
4. It leads to stronger relationships.
5. It leads to growth and profitability.

100/0 In 1998, the *Fortune* magazine named Synovus Bank as the 'most desirable' bank to work for in America. On walls, badges, and their desks, they had signs everywhere stating 100/0. Somebody asked the meaning of that sign. He was told that the '100' stands for hundred per cent responsibility. Nobody says, 'It's not my job.' Nobody says, 'I was late' or 'I got stuck in traffic'. A hundred per cent responsibility is taken by everyone for the success of the company. It is each one's responsibility to keep the company great.

Here '0' stands for zero excuses. It means that they give great service to every customer for every transaction. There is no excuse for not doing their best. Everybody is an ambassador for the organisation.

Holding someone accountable can also be unpleasant. Many times, we are afraid to hold others accountable. It appears like a let-down or a put down. People want to avoid friction as accountability can bring friction. When would it bring friction? It brings friction when one or both parties are not willing to accept responsibility and be accountable. That is where people feel let down and friction erupts. If we want to grow, the only way is to become accountable and to hold others accountable.

> *Not holding the incompetent accountable for their actions only brings an abundance of incompetence.*

Achievers Recognise That Big Pay Cheques And Lack Of Accountability Seldom Go Together.

ACTION PLAN

- Take a quick quiz to know your AQ (Accountability Quotient). Select the option that best suits your answer:

    i. I keep my commitments. | Always | Occasionally | Never |

    ii. People trust me. | Always | Occasionally | Never |

    iii. I learn from mistakes immediately. | Always | Occasionally | Never |

    iv. I take pride in my performance. | Always | Occasionally | Never |

    v. I don't shy away from my responsibility. | Always | Occasionally | Never |

    vi. I don't goof around. | Always | Occasionally | Never |

    vii. I understand other people's needs. | Always | Occasionally | Never |

    viii. I walk my talk. | Always | Occasionally | Never |

    ix. I help others achieve their goals. | Always | Occasionally | Never |

    x. I always call if I'm getting late. | Always | Occasionally | Never |

    xi. I make excuses for non-performance. | Always | Occasionally | Never |

    xii. I become defensive when I'm corrected. | Always | Occasionally | Never |

- From the above quiz, write down three ways you can improve your AQ.

    i. _____

    ii. _____

    iii. _____

CHAPTER 19

Take Ownership

" It is better to have one person working with us than a hundred people working for us — those who take ownership work with us, not for us. "

Take Ownership   Many years ago, I heard the story of a man named Steve who was working under the hot sun as a labourer of a company. A limousine stopped by and a man shouted, '*Steve come inside.*' Sitting in the limousine was John, the president of the company. Steve left all his work and sat inside the limousine. He exchanged pleasantries and had some cold water to drink. After a few minutes, they said goodbye to each other. Steve went back to work in the hot sun and John left. All Steve's co-workers were rather impressed and asked him enviously, 'How do you know John?' Steve replied, 'Not only do I know him, but both John and I started working together in this company, on the same day at the same position twenty-five years ago.' Everyone was left even more surprised. They asked Steve, 'How is it that both of you started working on the same day at the same position twenty-five years ago, and you are still working out in the hot sun and he has become the president of the company?' The answer Steve gave says it all. He said, 'Twenty-five years ago, John started working for the company and I started working for a dollar and twenty-eight cents an hour.' No wonder, John rose up to become the president and Steve was still working as a labourer. John took ownership. He had a larger picture in mind—he worked towards making the company grow bigger rather than making only himself grow. He understood that the more he contributed towards the growth of the company, the more he would grow.

Somebody might say that this kind of thing happens only in the western world, but that's really not true.

Five years ago, I met a person who had taken an early retirement from the defence services in India, and within a few years of starting his own business was making a turnover of a few hundred million dollars. One day a friend of his, who had also taken early retirement, came over looking for a job and asked if he could work with him. The owner said, *'Of course! I've known you for the last thirty years.'*

One day, after the office closed and everybody had gone home, the two friends sat talking to each other. The employee said to the owner, *'You remember, thirty years ago we both joined the services together on the same day?'* The owner said, *'Yes I remember.'* The man said,

'You were getting a thousand bucks, I was also getting a thousand bucks, you remember?' The owner said, 'Yes I remember.' Then he said, *'You were an employee then, I was an employee then. You remember?'* The owner said, 'Yes I remember.' Then the employee said, *'Look at this, thirty years later, I am still an employee and you are the owner of a company with a few hundred million dollars turnover. Isn't this luck?'* In my opinion, the reply that the owner gave is the crux of success.

The owner said, *'I didn't want to bring it up, but since you brought it up, I will address it. You may not like it, but you must hear it. I want to remind you of an incident that took place thirty years ago. We had had a long day and we walked two miles from the office to the barracks. It was nine-thirty at night. When we reached the barracks, it occurred to me that we had forgotten to switch off the light and the fan in the office. When I told you, what did you say? You said, "Don't you see what time it is? Isn't it late enough? Haven't we worked hard all day? Who's going to go back now to switch off the light and the fan? And if we do, it will be two miles going, two miles coming back and by the time we get back, it will be ten-thirty at night." You added, "What's the big deal? It is only one light. What's the big deal? It is only one fan. What's the big deal? It is only one night. And besides, what's the big deal, it belongs to the Government anyway. I'm not going back," and you went off to sleep. I went back to switch off the light and the fan and then I came back. Now listen to me carefully. Thirty years ago, we both joined the services together on the same day – that is correct. You were getting a thousand bucks and I was also getting a thousand bucks – that is also correct. You were an employee then, you are an employee now – that's also correct. But here's the difference…I was an owner that night thirty years ago and I'm an owner tonight too. And with the kind of thinking you have, you have lived the life of an employee and if you continue the same thinking, you will die an employee too.'* This is a true story.

What is the moral of this story?

The moral is very clear: Nobody ever becomes an owner or an employee based on a pay-cheque. A pay-cheque doesn't decide who is the owner or the employee. It is only the acceptance of ownership that decides the owner. Only when we feel like an owner within, do we behave like one. Our actions become those of an owner thereafter, and we take charge. A person who takes ownership, has a feeling of belonging. That means, 'I belong to the organisation and the organisation belongs to me.'

Whenever a person takes ownership, two things change drastically:

1. Their problem-solving ability, and
2. Their decision-making ability

What is leadership if not these two things put together?

The Feeling of Belonging Has it ever happened that you bought something from the store and something went wrong? You went back to the store and shouted at the person behind the counter. And the person said,

'Why do you shout at me? I only work here. I'm just an employee.'

When a person says, 'I only work here', what is he really saying? He is saying, *'I have no feeling of belonging. I only come here for a pay-cheque.'*

When an employee treats an employer only as a 'pay-cheque', he will never make a good employee. Similarly, when an employer treats an employee only as a 'money-making machine', he will never make a good employer either. There must be a feeling of belonging that binds them together. It's pretty common to see that **people who walk in for a few bucks will also walk out for a few bucks.**

The most important factor that brings a feeling of belonging is when people feel connected because of a meaningful purpose. For example, look at non-profit organisations such as The Rotary International, Lions Clubs International, The Red Cross, etc., who rely on an army of committed volunteers who put in both their time and funds to serve society for a cause.

Why? Because they take ownership and they have a feeling of belonging. People will do a lot for money. They will do more for a good leader. And they will do most for a belief.

Achievers Take Ownership And Become Unstoppable.

ACTION PLAN

- Evaluate your problem-solving ability and think of three ways to improve it.

    i. _____

    ii. _____

    iii. _____

- Evaluate your decision-making ability and note three things that will help you take better decisions.

    i. _____

    ii. _____

    iii. _____

- What three areas in your life could you take more ownership in?

    i. _____

    ii. _____

    iii. _____

CHAPTER 20

Tame Your Time

" Achievers think in terms of seconds and minutes, non-achievers think in terms of hours and days. "

I **wish I had more time** — I bet we all have said this at some point in our life.

- What if we had twenty-five hours in a day, or twenty-six?
- What would we do with those one or two extra hours?
- How would we utilise them?

Answering the above questions, please fill in the blank now.

_____

_____

If we go ahead and read this book without filling the blank space above, we will not benefit the way we should.

Myths about Time Management **M**yth One: Is there anything called time management? The answer is, 'no'. Why? Whenever we waste time, what are we wasting? We are wasting our lives. Most people don't waste time. They only waste their lives. **Time management is only a name given to life management**.

Myth Two: We keep hearing, 'Time comes and goes away.' Again, it is not true. Why? Because time is eternal. Time does not come and go away; we come and go away.

Time Wasted is Life Wasted **J**ust the way we can only do two things with money; Money can be used or abused, invested or spent. Invested money gives return, spent money is lost forever. Similarly, we can only do two things with time.

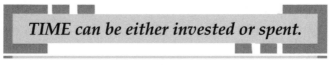

TIME can be either invested or spent.

Let us write down seven items each, that we consider invested or spent. For example:

Invested	Spent
1. Education and health	1. Unnecessary socialising
2. Skill and self-development	2. Idling away watching TV
3. Relationship building	3. Social media binge
4.	4.
5.	5.
6.	6.
7.	7.

> *If we waste time, time will waste us.*

Time is an equal opportunity **provider**. We all have exactly the same amount of time whether it is the president of the US, the prime minister of UK, the Chairman of IBM, or X Y Z, it doesn't matter. We all have exactly 168 hours a week. Every day we get a fresh bank balance of 86,400 seconds — we can either invest it or spend it.

Imagine, if every morning someone were to deposit a sum of $24 or $2,400 or $24,000 in our bank account with only one condition that we must spend or invest the entire amount within twenty-four hours and that we cannot carry forward the balance of whatever remains unused, what would we do? How would we respond? Since, the unused expires, would we not make every effort to use the entire balance most effectively within the stipulated time? Since you cannot carry forward, you want to optimise or else it is lost.

Each one of us is given a fresh deposit of twenty-four hours a day — no more, no less. It is up to us to use it, abuse it, or lose it. The funny part of time is that it has a uniform pace. No one can speed it, slow it, or stop it. The wealthiest person of the world cannot control it. If each moment is accounted for, then being committed and taking charge of our life is the only possible thing to do.

One Time **S**upposing you had a magic wand
Gift   and you were granted a wish that
             the next day you can have any car of
your choice, irrespective of the price — fully loaded
and totally complimentary. However, there is one
condition that this gift is only one-time. You can never
get a second car in your life. How would you want to
treat this car? Would you not:

1. Take care of this car.
2. Drive it carefully.
3. Make sure it doesn't get into the wrong hands.
4. Undertake timely maintenance and up-keeps.
5. Keep it protected from damage.
6. Abstain from driving after drinking.

The bottom line is that you would be proactive to
ensure the car's upkeep. You would maintain it and
avoid any damage. Now, if we would care so much
for a one-time expensive gift of a car, why wouldn't
we do the same thing for the one-time priceless gift
of life?

Peak   **O**nce a teacher demonstrated the
Performers   following example. He had four
                  items with him.

1. Big Stones   2. Small Pebbles
3. Sand   4. Water

He took a jar with a wide mouth and asked the
students to fit in all the four items in it. The students
tried different permutations and combinations but
they were not able to fit all the items in the jar. The

teacher then took over and demonstrated how it should have been done. He put the big stones first. He then poured small pebbles into the jar that occupied space between the stones. Next, he poured some sand that trickled down the stones and found its space. Last, he drizzled the water into the jar that easily seeped through the items. A little sand was left on the side. The teacher said, *'I realise a little sand did not fit in the jar but that doesn't matter.'*

Sand represents the little petty things in life. Things that we can do away with that really don't matter such as video games, being mad at people, and menial tasks. If we don't have time for them, who cares? The **small pebbles are the smaller priorities, things that matter, but are not necessarily important**. Things that can wait such as daily chores, hobbies, social dos, and socialising with people who are not really important, etc. The **big stones are the foundations of our lives** — the things that are important, that matter, that give us fulfilment and happiness. These are the things that money cannot buy such as our values, health, family, relationships, work life balance, continuous learning, things that we love, causes that we fight for, etc.

When the teacher was done a student asked, 'what does the water represent?' The teacher replied, 'no matter how full the jar appears, there is always room for a little more.'

> *If we lose time doing things that don't matter then we will not be left with time for the things that do matter.*

> *Four things never come back —*
> *a lost opportunity, a spoken word,*
> *a fired bullet and a wasted moment.*

What Do We Do With Our Lives?

Supposing our life span was eighty years. Look at how we, approximately, spend it:

- Twenty-six years sleeping.   (8 hours a day × 80)
- Ten years socialising with friends and family.

    (3 hours a day × 80)

- Three-and-a-half years of eating.

    (1 hour a day × 80)

- Six months of waiting at traffic signals.

    (15 minutes a day × 80)

- Ten years of watching TV and looking at technological gadgets.   (3 hours a day × 80)
- Nine years on phone calls. (2.75 hours a day × 80)
- Four years on house work. (1.2 hours a day × 80)
- Four years waiting in line or looking for misplaced objects.   (1.2 hours a day × 80)
- Four years of miscellaneous activities that covers sickness, vacations, etc.   (1.2 hours a day × 80)
- Nine years left of working time.

    (2.8 hours a day × 80)

The above is an approximation and may vary from person to person, but it does get us thinking about re-evaluating our priorities in life.

Time is More Precious Than Money If we were eighty years of age today, going forward, there would not be much time left. What are the things which 'we could have', 'should have', or 'would have' done more? Those are words of regret. Life is a one-way street — we can only go forward, we cannot turn back. **Life does not come with a rewind button either.**

Time is a perishable commodity and management is the handling of time. Our time on this earth is finite. It is limited. The clock keeps ticking and things keep changing. We all have choices and decisions to make. Success or failure in life depends on our ability and/or inability to manage time. Mismanagement of time leads to stress. Lack of priorities leads to lack of focus and disorientation, which in turn leads to chaos.

Some of the greatest achievers in the world had the same amount of time that we have, but they used it well and that is what made them perform at their peak. Time cannot be manufactured. It cannot be used quickly or slowly. It cannot be borrowed or lent. It appears to pass quickly when we are enjoying ourselves and it drags when we feel trapped.

To accomplish anything we need time. Whenever there is loss of time, the loss is permanent. Time is irreplaceable and hence indispensable. What we do with our time — use, abuse, or lose, is up to us. It cannot be stored or saved, accumulated or carried forward. The better the usage of time, the greater the accomplishment and the more rewarding is life.

Unfortunately, people forget the obvious; the one thing that cannot be recycled is wasted time. Once gone, it is gone forever.

Remember, time is more precious than money. We need to ask ourselves whether we're spending or investing time. One day well utilised is a day gained, which means a day well-invested. One day poorly utilised is a day lost, which means a day spent and gone forever.

I do not care what philosophy one believes in, we have got only one shot at this game called life. **This life is not a dress rehearsal and the stakes are too high**. Unlike the game of football, where we can replace players, in the game of life, we have to play our own game.

Why is time more precious than money?

- Time invested can create money, money invested cannot create time.
- Money can be borrowed, stolen or transferred; time cannot be bought, sold, traded or transferred.
- Money can go and come back. Time cannot.
- Money can be gifted, but time cannot be.
- Money fluctuates, time does not.
- We can measure money-balance till the last penny, but time-balance cannot be measured. Nobody knows how much time-balance we are left with.

> *Time teaches us the value of life,*
> *Life teaches us the value of time.*

What is the Value of Time?

To realise the value of **ONE YEAR**,
ask a student who failed a grade.

To realise the value of **ONE MONTH**,
ask a mother who gave birth to a premature baby.

To realise the value of **ONE DAY**,
ask the person who was born on 29 February.

To realise the value of **ONE HOUR**,
ask a person who waited for his lover.

To realise the value of **ONE MINUTE**,
ask a person who missed the train.

To realise the value of **ONE MILLI-SECOND**,
ask the person who won a silver medal
in the Olympics.

— Anonymous

Some major time wasters to avoid are as follows:

1. Indecision

2. Procrastination

3. Poor organisation or being disorganised

4. Lack of priorities

5. Lack of planning or improper planning

6. Unplanned interruptions

7. Faulty implementation leading to loss, duplication or damage control

8. Avoidable or careless mistakes

9. Unnecessary or ineffective meetings

10. Constant firefighting or crisis handling

11. No delegation or ineffective delegation

12. Lack of clarity of roles and goals (lack of focus)

13. Unnecessary and poor use of travel time

14. Waiting time

15. Poor Communication

All time wasters fall into these two categories:

1. Either they are self-generated — within our control, or

2. Beyond our control — this could be external or unforeseen.

Self-generated time wasters are internal and result from the following:

•   Lack of planning

•   Lack of discipline

•   Lack of confidence

•   Lack of high self-esteem

An example of an unforeseen (beyond one's control) time waster could be:

A tree collapses in the middle of the road leading to a traffic jam. Now you are trapped and cannot reach your destination on time.

Procrastination One of the major time wasters is **Procrastination**.

> *Procrastination steals time, destroys initiative, and ruins lives.*

Unjustified postponement is called **procrastination,** which means 'not doing what is important', that which **could be** done, **should be** done and **ought to be** done. Not doing what ought to be done is unjustified and irresponsible behaviour. It is the practice of doing what's easy and pleasurable rather than what is important.

Justified Postponement is not called procrastination such as:

1. I'm waiting for information so I cannot prepare my report. Or,
2. The doctor is waiting for blood reports so he cannot start the treatment.

If **something could be done** but we didn't do it, it is **careless behaviour.**

If **something should be done** but we are not doing it, it is **stubbornness.**

Why Do People Procrastinate?

A major cause why people procrastinate is because of their escapist behaviour. They don't have the courage to face up to the situation. Hence, they keep postponing. The more they keep postponing, the higher the price tag, the greater the loss.

There could be various reasons for postponing things:

1. Irresponsible behaviour
2. Lack of focus
3. Avoiding an unpleasant task

4. Lack of priority
5. Doing what is easy rather than what is important
6. Indecisive behaviour
7. Fear of failure
8. Being depressed or demotivated
9. Nothing to look forward to in life
10. Fatigue
11. Casual approach
12. Not giving due importance to essential things
13. Forgetfulness or just plain laziness could be other reasons amid a range of them.
14. Inertia

A BIG obstacle is **inertia** or not getting started. Disinterest to even begin a certain task is one of the prime factors of procrastination.

Indecision and Procrastination Indecision and procrastination steal time, drain energy, and ruin lives. Most people don't realise that the energy required to procrastinate is much greater than the energy required to do the job. Delayed or deferred decisions can reduce productivity and have a compounding effect.

When we procrastinate what we are really doing is postponing the things that need to be done in a timely manner.

> *Completing work energises us whereas leaving work incomplete drains our energy.*

Do You Know the Cost of Procrastination?

It's huge!

- **On finances**
- **On health**
- **On relationships**
- **On developing skills**

The compounding effect of the neglect of all of the above is massive.

How to Overcome Procrastination?

Are we permanent under-performers or under-achievers because we keep postponing things in life? If so, then here are some steps that will help us overcome the negative habit:

- Step 1. Awareness and recognition of the habit
- Step 2. Evaluation of the cost—physically, financially, and mentally
- Step 3. Decide and commit to get rid of it
- Step 4. Overcome inertia and get started

The saddest words in life are:

- It might have been...
- I should have...
- I could have...
- I wish I had...
- If only I had given a little extra...

> *'Never leave till tomorrow,*
> *which you can do today.'*
> — *Benjamin Franklin*

I am sure all achievers wanted to procrastinate, but never got around to it. When someone says, 'I will do it one of these days,' we can be sure it means 'none of these days.'

If we're waiting for all lights to turn green before we leave home, then let us stay home. Why? Because they will never all turn green, and we'll never leave home. That will never happen and we fail even before we start.

Make a Habit of Doing It Now

He slept beneath the moon
He basked beneath the sun
He lived a life of going to do
And died with nothing done.

– James Albery

Stop Procrastinating: Isn't It Time That We Put Off 'Putting Off'?

ACTION PLAN

- Please rate yourself on the following time wasters on a scale of 1–10 (1 being the least and 10 being the highest):

    i. Indecision `1 2 3 4 5 6 7 8 9 10`

    ii. Procrastination `1 2 3 4 5 6 7 8 9 10`

    iii. Poor organisation or being disorganised `1 2 3 4 5 6 7 8 9 10`

    iv. Lack of priorities `1 2 3 4 5 6 7 8 9 10`

    v. Lack of planning or improper planning `1 2 3 4 5 6 7 8 9 10`

    vi. Unplanned interruptions `1 2 3 4 5 6 7 8 9 10`

    vii. Faulty implementation leading to loss, duplication or damage control `1 2 3 4 5 6 7 8 9 10`

    viii. Avoidable or careless mistakes `1 2 3 4 5 6 7 8 9 10`

    ix. Unnecessary or ineffective meetings `1 2 3 4 5 6 7 8 9 10`

    x. Constant firefighting or crisis handling `1 2 3 4 5 6 7 8 9 10`

    xi. No delegation or ineffective delegation `1 2 3 4 5 6 7 8 9 10`

    xii. Lack of clarity of roles and goals `1 2 3 4 5 6 7 8 9 10`

    xiii. Unnecessary and poor use of travel time `1 2 3 4 5 6 7 8 9 10`

    xiv. Time wasted waiting `1 2 3 4 5 6 7 8 9 10`

    xv. Poor communication `1 2 3 4 5 6 7 8 9 10`

- Make a list of your priorities in life, then set your goals accordingly.

  i. _____

  ii. _____

  iii. _____

  iv. _____

  v. _____

- Evaluate the cost. Five years down the line what do you think would be the damaging effects of procrastination on your:

  i. Health _____

  ii. Work _____

  iii. Family _____

  iv. Intellect _____

  v. Emotions _____

  vi. Social life _____

  vii. Finance _____

- What three actions do you commit to that will help you manage your time better?

  i. _____

  ii. _____

  iii. _____

CHAPTER 21

Be Proactive —Make It Happen!

" The greatest achievement of a person in his lifetime is not measured by what he got, but by what he became. "

A Go-Giver or A Go-Getter? In 1985, Bob Munro volunteered his time to go and serve in the poorest slums of Africa on behalf of the United Nations. He loved football. One day, he was passing through the Mathare slums in Nairobi, Kenya, which happens to be one of the poorest areas in the world, and where more than a quarter million people live in abject poverty and filth. He saw some children playing football, bare feet, in total dirt and filth — they weren't actually playing football, but kicking each other. As he saw one of the children kick the other, he immediately shouted, 'Foul', and the game stopped. He got out of his car and being the white man, obviously stood out. As an ardent lover of football, he said, *'This is not the way to play football.'* He took the ball and told the boys, *'Tomorrow I will bring another ball and teach you how to play football.'* The next day, 600 children were there to play football. He made a rule that only those children who clean up the place be allowed to play. He started a volunteers' group for self-help and said, *'Those who want to play football as part of my team must clean up.'* The children got involved and started cleaning the slums, and out of love for football, slowly the entire area was cleaned. As time went by, he developed teams to play. He developed referees from within. Guess what was the result in four years?

The Kenyan football eleven national team emerged from the same Mathare slums. Bob Munro has created thousands of football teams from there, but the rules are very unique. The rules are very clear that every player in those football teams must contribute 60 hours to social work and community service per month. Only then can they play football. They get additional points not for winning a game, but for completing a community service project such as cleaning, counselling and helping others. He has created 8,000 volunteers out of this system of community service through the love of football.

The rules of the game are quite interesting. If there is an argument or difference of opinion, only the captain speaks and the rest must remain silent and obey. If anybody misbehaves, the team loses regardless of the score. The players are literally responsible for the behaviour of the whole team. Prize rules are even more interesting. The only award is not a trophy, but scholarships for hundred children that have to be donated among the community. This has been going on for the last twenty years. What an inspirational message. What a way to live!

Mathare valley has won two environmental awards for keeping the valley clean. These children are probably not college graduates, but they have the motivation to be proactive and serve society. Munro made the absolute impossible happen by being proactive. Not only did he transform the area, but he showed them a way of life. He created a whole team of proactive people.

> ### Be proactive and
> ### make the impossible happen!

Cardinal rule to live by: If we want to live a happy and fulfilling life, then we must always help when ever we can help someone. When we can help but we do not, we never feel good about ourselves. By not helping, we live with a feeling of guilt and regret.

Learn to respond, not react. Be proactive, not reactive. When we take a medication prescribed by a doctor, the doctor asks, *'What is the outcome?'* If we say that it's causing a reaction, he'll ask us to stop consumption right away as it's dangerous. But if we say, we are responding well, he'll ask us to continue with the medicine. Being proactive and responsive are both positive traits.

Become Proactive — What is Goodness? If we take a survey, and ask people, 'Are you good?' Most people would respond with a 'yes'. Ask them, 'What makes you good?' and the responses will be:

- I don't cheat, so I'm good.
- I don't lie, so that makes me good.
- I don't steal, so I'm good.

If we analyse the above rationales, there is not much substance in them. Just think of the person who says, '*I don't cheat*'. Well, that only means that he is not a cheat, but that doesn't make him good.

And the person who says, '*I don't lie*', only means he is not a liar, but that doesn't make him good either.

A person who says, '*I don't steal*', only means that he is not a thief, but that also doesn't make him good. **A person becomes good when he actually does good rather than not doing wrong.**

Go ask a medical doctor, he will tell us that **absence of ill health does not mean good health.** Similarly, absence of faults does not make a person good. A person only becomes good when he actually does good. That is called **being pro-active.**

Achievers Are Go-Getters — They Make Things Happen!

ACTION PLAN

- Write down three instances where you were reactive, and going forward would become proactive:

    i. _____

    ii. _____

    iii. _____

You Are The
CEO Of Your Life.
Take Decisions Befitting
Your Position

CHAPTER 22

Make Decisions

In order to get started effectively in the journey of life we need to define:

1. Our values
2. The quality of life for which we need to take wise decisions

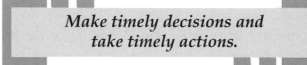

Make timely decisions and take timely actions.

Before we take any decision in life we should clarify the following three things:

1. The rules of the game

2. The stakes involved

3. The time to quit – when to exit

More important than the decision is the decision making process. Why? Because if the process is right, the chances are that a majority of your decisions will go right.

> *Standing up for something and*
> *sitting down both take courage, but*
> *knowing when to do so takes wisdom.*

Maturity of Decision-Making Ability

Why is there so much of disparity in compensation in any organisation?

The disparity of compensation exists **not because of the hours we put in, but because of the maturity of our decision-making ability.**

There were two friends who went to school together. When they grew up one of them became the prime minister to the king and the other became a boatman. The boatman always felt jealous of the prime minister, especially because they went to the same school and, at one time, were colleagues. He used to justify his resentment by asking, *'What qualification does the prime minister have that I don't? Why is he the prime minister and I only a boatman in spite of the same academic qualifications?'* He was always jealous.

Once the king decided to go to the forest for his annual strategic planning meeting. They had to cross the river. The king picked this man's boat. All through the time that the boatman rowed his boat, in his heart he kept resenting the prime minister for being with the king. They reached the other side of the river and set up the camp. At night, they all retired to their respective tents. Suddenly, from the darkness, the king heard a cry. He came out, saw the boatman sitting next to the fire and asked him to check what the cry was about. The boatman went over, saw that there was a cat, came back and informed the king about the same. The king asked, *'What kind of a cat is it? A domestic or a wild cat?'* The boatman said, *'I didn't check on that, I'll go back and find out.'* So he checked, came back and said *'It's a domestic cat.'* The king asked, *'Why is it crying?'* The boatman said, *'I don't know. I didn't check on that. I'll go and check.'* He went again, came back and said, *'The cat has given kittens.'* The king asked, *'How many kittens?'* The boatman said, *'I didn't count. I didn't check on that. I'll go and check.'* He checked and came back and said, *'It's given four kittens.'* The king asked, *'What colour were they?'* Same reply, *'I didn't check. I'll go check and come back.'* So he came back this time and said, *'There are two black and two white.'* The king asked, *'What colour is the cat.'* He said, *'I didn't check.'* Again the same thing happened. He came back and said the cat is half-black and half-white. The king asked, *'What have you done about it?'* He said, *'Nothing. I'll just go and do something now.'* At this point, the king stopped him. He said, *'You stand here now and watch.'* He called his prime minister and told him to find out what the cry was about. The prime minister went, came back and said, *'My Lord, there is a domestic cat, half black and half white, who has given four kittens – two black and two white. They are feeding on their mother and there is enough food for the cat as well. I've blocked the place so that the cat is comfortable on the other side and does not come over to our side. Please go to sleep. Regardless, I will keep a watch on it anyway.'* The king only said one thing to the boatman, *'All the while that you were rowing the boat*

to bring us here, I could sense your feelings of resentment.
Now do you realise why he is my prime minister and you
are not? The difference is that what you could not do in
several trips, in spite of being instructed, he's done in one
single trip!'

The maturity of your decision-making ability
determines whether or not you would reach a certain
position in life.

Assumptions Once the Chairman of a billion
Mess Up dollar company was to hire
Decisions a CEO. After the initial screening
process and series of interviews,
their HR Head shortlisted one person who was well
qualified in his opinion. The stage was set for him to
get the letter of appointment. It was customary for the
Chairman to hand over the letter at a special lunch.
After they were seated comfortably, they both ordered
soup. When the soup was served, the prospective CEO
started sprinkling salt on his soup without tasting it.
The lunch got over and nobody spoke about the letter
of appointment. They shook hands and parted with
the Chairman's words, *'Our HR will be in touch.'* Upon
his return, the Chairman informed the HR Head that
the candidate was rejected. Everyone was surprised,
but who could question the Chairman's decision? The
HR Head, out of inquisitiveness, asked the Chairman
just so he could understand the reason for the rejection
of the preferred candidate. The Chairman narrated
the entire incident of the luncheon meeting and said,
'I question the maturity of the decision-making ability of a

person who would add salt without first tasting his food. Why would a person do that? What kind of decision is this? I can understand somebody adding salt after tasting his soup, but I cannot understand adding salt without tasting it. This just shows that he took a decision without getting his facts right in the first place. The question is, is he the kind of person we want to head our organisation? If so, then we are heading for disaster.' The HR Head asked, *'Do such little things matter?'* The Chairman said, *'Do you really think this is little? If this is little in your opinion, you should be the next to go.'*

The moral of the Chairman's message is very clear:

1. **Get your facts right before taking a decision.**
2. **Do not make assumptions as this impairs your decision-making ability.**

Every morning we wake up and whether we realise it or not, we make hundreds of decisions including which side of the bed we want to get off from, what clothes we want to wear, what breakfast to eat, which route to take to the office, etc.

Why don't people take decisions? It's due to the fear of making a mistake or taking a wrong decision. Hence, they maintain a status quo, or in other words, do nothing. They become inactive not realising that, in life, we are not only penalised for our actions, but also our inactions. Indecision leads to inaction. Whether we realise it or not, indecision is also a decision by default. I decide not to decide. **The window of opportunity does not remain open forever. It requires the right decision at the right time.**

Indecision is called mental paralysis, which comes out of lack of confidence, non-committal nature and sitting on the fence. A successful life is full of decisions.

A journalist asked a very successful business executive, *'What is the secret of your success?'* He said, *'Two words – good decisions.'* Then the journalist asked, *'How did you learn how to make good decisions?'* The business tycoon said, *'One word – experience.'* So the journalist asked, *'How did you get the experience to make good decisions?'* He said, *'Two words – bad decisions.'*

Successful people don't look to avoid making decisions. When we take ownership, decision making becomes easier.

> **A good worker doesn't necessarily mean he is a good decision-maker.**

The Worst Kind of Decision is Indecision

A farmer had a very good hard-working person at his potato farm. This worker had the highest output, hence the farmer got impressed and promoted him to the level of a supervisor. Now, as a supervisor, this person's role was to segregate the potatoes in three categories based on their quality from the highest, to the medium and the lowest. The farmer did his explanation to get the worker started hoping for the similar output at the end of the day. To his surprise in the evening, this worker was still sitting with the same heap of potatoes that he had in the morning with nothing done. The farmer asked the reason. The worker said, '*I am pretty confused; I'm not able to decide which one goes where.*'

The above story makes one thing clear that working hard is one thing, whereas decision making is another. The worker toiled the whole day, let it go waste, but couldn't move one potato. Maybe, he was nervous about taking a wrong decision. His inability to make a decision resulted in a total loss.

What sometimes prevents people in taking decisions is being over cautious. People who are overcautious are also averse to risks not realising that everything in life is a risk.

- When we were born, it was a risk.
- If we think action is risky, try inaction and see how risky that is.
- Investing is risky, but try not investing, it's twice as risky.
- Getting married is risky, having kids is risky, not getting married is risky, and not having kids is risky.

What is not risky? Nothing in life.

When should one take a risk in life? Only when these three elements are present:

1. When the upside is open, big and lucrative.
2. The downside is limited and one can sustain the loss.
3. The odds are in one's favour and the likelihood of success is great.

People may suffer from inaction. Responsibility and prompt action go together. The objective of taking a courageous stand is to resolve challenges rather than prolong indecision. Some people want to go through life playing it safe, hoping they will make it to death, safely. They are living dead bodies. We need to learn to live by this philosophy: **Live while you are alive**. It is not only the length of our lives that matter, but the quality of our lives and how we live them.

People who suffer from inaction, keep asking before taking a decision, 'What if…' They are stuck in that 'what if trap', and they do nothing. They get into a mode of inaction and become paralysed. It doesn't mean that a person should be foolishly reckless. Opportunity only knocks once. The next one may be better or worse, but never the same one. That's why it is crucial to make the right decision at the right time. When we are hit by a car, that's not the time to do SWOT Analysis or evaluate the specs of the car. **That is a time for damage control.**

Once You Make A Decision, Nature Conspires To Help You Achieve More.

ACTION PLAN

- Think of three instances where you made assumptions and they proved to be incorrect.

    i. _____

    ii. _____

    iii. _____

- Learning from the above mistakes, write down three ways in which you would want to rectify your decision-making ability:

    i. _____

    ii. _____

    iii. _____

If We Want To Leave A Legacy, Then Either Do Something Worth Writing Or Write Something Worth Doing

CHAPTER 23

Leave a Legacy

There are **two kinds of people** in this world:
1. Those who remember names
2. Those whose names are worth remembering

> *Our ancestors give us our name*
> *but respect comes only from*
> *our behaviour.*

Money, fame and power are important, but they can only buy expensive toys and boost your ego and nothing more. It is really your legacy that counts.

How much did Steve Jobs leave? Answer is – ALL OF IT!

How much did Roosevelt leave? Answer is – ALL OF IT!

How much will Warren Buffet and Bill Gates leave? Answer is – ALL OF IT!

> *A man's life is not measured by its length*
> *but its depth and how well it is spent.*
> *Actors make an impression,*
> *great people make an impact.*

Be Sung about after You Go Once an elderly man, named Johnson, died. In fact, he was the oldest man in the village. To pay tribute to him, a local journalist wanted to write something about him in his newspaper. Since the deceased had not done anything worthwhile that could be called an accomplishment, he just wrote *'Mr Johnson really had not done anything terribly bad or wrong. He was not a drunkard nor had he gone to jail.'*

Honouring the Dishonourable Once a very corrupt criminal politician died—there was no person in town who he had not harmed in some form or the other. There was a huge procession following his dead body to perform the last rites. A man passing by, saw the unusually large crowd, stopped and asked one of the persons, *'Don't you know the reputation of this man who died? He was the biggest disgrace to humanity. Why are you all going to perform the last rites because such gatherings only take place out of respect to a noble soul?'* The man replied, *'You're totally right. But all of us are going to the funeral not to pay any respect, but to make sure that he is actually dead.'*

Someone once said, **'I have never killed anyone, but there are few funerals that I have attended and really enjoyed.'**

What a legacy! Is that the way to live or is that the way to die?

A crook died and at the funeral the minister, who was reading the eulogy said, *'John was a great guy, a wonderful husband, a terrific father, and an honourable man.'* The widow quickly called the son and said, *'Son just check that there is no mix up in the caskets.'*

Mark Twain once said, *'I didn't attend the funeral, but I sent a nice letter saying I approve of it.'*

In a corrupt system, decorating and giving awards to the unworthy becomes a common practice. It may be a way of rewarding the sycophants. The deserving remain deprived because they don't have a godfather. The question arises, what kind of a culture is this? What examples are we setting for the coming generations?

Traitor Honoured Until the late 1950s, the growth rate of the Philippines' economy was one of the highest in East Asia. However, under President Ferdinand Marcos' leadership from 1965 to 1986, the Philippines 'slipped behind other countries in the region'. With its abundance of natural resources such as timber, coconuts, sugar, bananas, rubber, and minerals, and its literate and hard-working labour force, the Philippines should have been one of Asia's most prosperous economies today. But it became 'one of the worst performing economies' among the ASEAN.

- Carmen Navarro Pedrosa had estimated that President Marcos amassed a staggering $15 billion, which was more than half of the country's national debt.

  Senior Minister of Singapore, Lee Kuan Yew observed, 'Only in the Philippines could a leader like Ferdinand Marcos, who looted his county for over 20 years, still be considered for a national burial. Insignificant amounts of the loot had been recovered, yet his wife and children were allowed to return and engage in politics. General Fabian Ver, Marcos's commander-in-chief, had fled the Philippines together with Marcos in 1986. When he died in Bangkok, the Estrada government gave the general military honours at his burial.'[1]

Isn't there something wrong with the values of a nation that can honour a traitor, who has looted the nation, instead of putting him in jail? Aren't we witnessing similar or even worse behaviour in the third world countries? No wonder, they are called third world, because they behave third class.

When a corrupt politician dies, his name should not appear in the Obituary column. Rather, it should appear in the Public Improvement column in newspapers.

---

[1] *http://globalbalita.com/2011/01/10/lee-kuan-yew-on-filipinos-and-the-philippines/*

Have a Vision!

What's a Vision? Vision is the ability to see the invisible. If we can see the invisible, we can achieve the impossible. All great achievers had a vision as well as the ability to see the invisible. Vision is the starting point for any accomplishment.

> *A visionary person is the one who can see what others cannot.*

People with narrow vision can never be large-hearted. People with narrow spirits can never achieve big things in life.

It is said that Walt Disney wanted to create the Disney World in Orlando, USA. Construction went full steam ahead, but before the opening, Walt Disney died. On the opening day, two of the executives were talking between themselves and one said, *'Too bad Walt Disney is not alive to see all this.'* The other replied, *'He already saw all this, that's why you and I are here.'* That's the power of vision.

It is so appropriately said that, 'where there is no vision people shall perish.' Humanity owes its progress to the visionaries who had great ideas and left legacies. Scientists, artists, poets, and philosophers are the architects of the world. They enrich the world through their lives. Without their efforts, humanity would be a lot poorer.

Those who harbour a lofty vision will someday convert it into reality.

Sadly, many people have vision, but they never act on it. Hence, **vision without action is hallucination, vision with action is conviction.**

• Michelangelo, the great Italian sculptor, had the vision of the statue of David.
• Lee Kuan Yew, the first prime-minister of Singapore, had the vision of a prosperous nation.
• Buddha, founder of Buddhism, had the vision of a spiritual and peaceful world.

We must cherish and nurture our vision and make every effort to translate it into reality.

The potential of a giant tree is hidden in a small seed. Similarly, the manifestation of reality starts from a lofty vision. The person who has a clear vision and purpose, with a definite action plan cannot be stopped. A dreamer has to go beyond his dream; he must also be a doer. Some people just dream of great accomplishments while others stay awake and do them.

In 1960 John Kennedy said, '*We will put a man on the moon within this decade.*' Guess what the reaction was? People said, '*It cannot be done.*' It was called unrealistic. It had never been done by anyone before. In fact, one of the scientists went as far as to say that it takes several million decisions, activities, and co-ordination to do that. There were enough reasons not to even try, forget doing. But Kennedy thought differently. He felt that the US had the opportunity to be the first. People said, '*We have no resources.*' Kennedy said, '*Let's become resourceful.*' Kennedy's vision and commitment were so big and strong that it mobilised the entire scientific community to do whatever was needed to turn his vision into reality.

Live in the Present but with a Vision of the Future We need to enjoy our present moments because these are the only ones we can live in. We need to enjoy the gifts we have — our health, family, friends and our work. At the same time, while enjoying the gifts, one needs to move in the right direction to ensure a brighter future.

For over half a century, the Swiss were the leading watch manufacturers in the world. In the mid-sixties, the digital technology was introduced and patented by the Swiss, but the watch making industry rejected it in favour of the traditional technology, which comprised of ball-bearing, gear and main springs. They did not see the writing on the wall that the world was ready for something new. Seiko, a Japanese company, had the vision to foresee the future and picked up the digital patent and literally became the world's leading watch manufacturing company overnight. Almost 80 per cent of the watch manufacturers went out of business overnight in Switzerland till Swatch watches, a Swiss company, recognised the opportunity, caught up, and regained its market share.

> *A far-sighted vision has the ability to see beyond the obvious.*

Why would a farmer plough the field and plant the seed if he could not see the results of the harvest?

Vision is the ability to see the things that don't exist today. Every building was seen in a vision before it became a physical reality. We can't just start laying bricks without having a clear picture of the building. If somebody asks, 'What are you doing?' We can't say, 'I don't know.'

If it cannot be seen mentally, then it can never translate into physical reality. When should we start building the physical structure? Only when we finish seeing it mentally.

> *Winners live every day as if it were their last day because one of these days it's going to be, and they don't know which one it's going to be. But when they leave, they leave as winners.*

The Memoir **M**ost people fear that life will come to an end, but unfortunately for some it never begins. Reaching our potential doesn't only amount to helping ourselves but also serves a bigger purpose, which is serving the world.

Mr Smith, an elderly teacher who had been teaching John, his favourite student the principles of success for a few years told him, *'Please come for the last principle next week.'* As per schedule, John showed up on time and rang the bell. It was the teacher's daughter who opened the door. John asked if Mr Smith was home. The daughter said sadly, *'He just passed away last week. He is no more, but you must be John.'* John said, *'Yes, I am.'* His daughter said, *'My dad left a letter for you. Please come inside and read it.'* John was escorted to the library, of the big mansion, where Mr Smith used to read and write. John opened the letter and started reading. It reads as follows:

Dear John,

If you are reading this message, obviously it means I am physically gone forever, but in spirit, I shall always be with you. I wanted to share with you the final principle of success personally but that's the way life is. We are not on this planet permanently. I learnt from a wise man that if you want to leave a legacy, do something worth writing or write something worth doing. In other words, a meaningful life must be purposeful. Just like a great book has a great binding thread or a theme, great men have a deep hunger for purpose. Good human beings never die, they only depart. They live forever through their good deeds. Rascals die and that's good riddance to bad rubbish.

Life is short, but if it is lived well, it is good. It seems like yesterday when I was a kid playing with my friends; we fought over little things only to realise later that they didn't really matter. I got married when I was twenty-two to a wonderful lady who literally changed my life. I am blessed that she came into my life. Friends asked me if getting married at twenty-two wasn't a little too early. My answer was, if I had a rewind button to my life, I would get married two years earlier to the same lady. I am blessed with two lovely daughters and grand children who I hope would be proud of their heritage.

I was born with a silver spoon as my family had coal mines that were later nationalised and then we literally came on the street. I started life afresh washing cars, going door-to-door with a bucket in my hand for two years. Gradually, I got into selling vacuum cleaners and moved onto selling life insurance. God was kind. I got into three businesses, bought a company out of California and started operations in New Jersey with no clients. Eventually, I sold my company with almost 500 clients. I learnt one thing— **there is no substitute for hard work.**

I did well for myself but I could have done better had I remained focused. I made a lot of money and lost a lot too. But more than money what I lost out on was the memories that I could have and should have created for my family. I kept thinking that I will be a different person tomorrow, but tomorrow never came. I kept thinking I will retire early, but never did.

I always felt that time was on my side. I was young and I had all the time left, but how foolish I was that I couldn't see what was so obvious. I never realised that time does not come and go away, we come and go away. We can always measure bank balances to the last penny, but nobody knows how much time balance we are left with. I learnt the hard way that **time teaches us the value of life and life teaches us the value of time. If we waste time, time will waste us.**

These are two events over which we have no control—when we come into this world and when we leave it; but what we do in between is our choice. How well we have lived is determined by what legacy we leave for those who follow us.

When I started my career, I was lost till somebody showed me the direction that changed my life. From that day onwards, I learnt that there is no self-made man. Every life we touch, we either strengthen or weaken them. I learnt that for any degree of success that we achieve, somebody somewhere has made some contribution to it.

My purpose in life has been to enrich the lives of those who come after me and leave this world a better place than I found. So, I decided to become a teacher and share with others the principles of success. But most important, every day that I taught, I learnt a little more. I realised that the person who ends up teaching ends up learning the most. I also learnt that it is a lot easier to preach than to practice, but every day I made every effort to practise what I taught. I learnt that we need to walk our talk. In doing so, we gain credibility.

John, remember that positive thinkers have always been in minority; but they have always been a one-man army. Whenever change has been brought, it has always been brought about by one person. The masses never brought change. They always followed.

Most people die before they are dead. They waste their lives and when they realise they don't have much time left, they regret it. I don't care what philosophy you believe in, we've got this one shot at this game called life and the stakes are too high. There is no rewind button. This life is not a dress rehearsal. Unlike the game of football, where you can replace players, in the game of life, you have to play your own game.

*The one thing that is clear is that there are only **two choices in life—you can either live by design or live*** *by default.* *Many people live their lives like robots. They go to work, come back, with no vision in their lives; but before they realise it, their end comes. Their dreams remain unfulfilled, and eventually they become nightmares.*

*John, remember, **winners don't do different things, they do things differently**. The earlier you start in life the better you are. You are young. You have a whole life ahead of you. You can achieve great heights if you live by design, not by default. Unfortunately, **most people die with the music still in them. They haven't lived while they were alive.***

If you design your life based on the principles of success, you will live a purposeful and meaningful life. *You will live an exemplary life. People will quote you as an example. You will become a role model. Parents will be happy to name their children after you. **Don't ask how many people know you or how many you know. Ask, are you worth knowing?***

If others want to live a petty life, let them. But not you. Why? Because you are my student.

*John, **every seed has the potential of starting a forest.** You plant a tree, it will give more seeds, which will help your future generations to plant more trees.*

*Remember, one more cardinal rule to live by, and that is, **when you can help others, you must, or you will never feel good about yourself. Feeling good is a natural outcome of doing good and doing good is a natural outcome of being good.***

John, turn your potential into reality. My life became more fulfilled once I started teaching the principles of success to people like you. So in turn you can further teach the principles of success to the coming generations. Make teaching a passion.

John, you are like my son. I feel privileged to have met you and shared with you what I learnt from people much wiser than me. You have actually done me a big favour by being my student. You made me a teacher. Without you, I could not have left a legacy.

*John, **values are priceless. The moment you put a price tag on values, they lose value.***

*Remember **that losers count their days, winners make their days count.***

John, make each day count.

Love,

Your Teacher,

Mr Smith

(The above letter reflects my life and carries my sentiments for my children and coming generations.)

ACTION PLAN

- Identify three things you would like to be remembered for:

    i. _____

    ii. _____

    iii. _____

- Write down three actions you commit to take to leave a legacy:

    i. _____

    ii. _____

    iii. _____

INTERNATIONAL BESTSELLERS

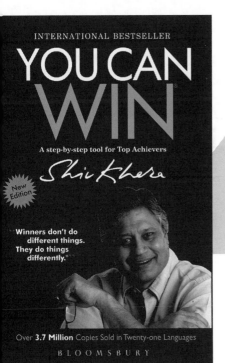

- Optimize Performance

- Accelerate Success

- Avoid Pitfalls

Increase Sales

Turn a No into Yes

Improve Bottom Line

GAIN & RETAIN CUSTOMERS

YOU®
CAN
WIN

GROW BY INCREASING SALES AND PRODUCTIVITY

2 Day Program

Mastering Selling Skills

TURN NOs INTO YESes

- Overcome resistance, build trust and close more sales
- Gain confidence and make dynamic sales presentations
- Distinguish between transactional selling and relationship selling
- Learn the Dos and DON'Ts of professional selling
- Learn to become effective negotiator Build Customer Loyalty

UNLEASH YOUR POTENTIAL

- Increase Sales by Identifying buying motives and selling opportunities
- Meet and exceed customers' expectations

WHO SHOULD ATTEND

Those who want to grow professionally by making selling as their career or veteran who want to sharpen their skills and excel in Selling.

Shiv Khera

MAKE POWERFUL SPEECHES & PRESENTATIONS

BE LOOKED UP AS
AN EXPERT IN YOUR FIELD

YOU® CAN WIN

2 Day Program

Public Speaking & Presentation Skills

GAIN RESPECT

- Gain confidence to face any audience
- Overcome stage fright
- Develop your natural speaking style
- Address questions in hostile situations
- Deliver impromptu speeches and think on your feet

GAIN A COMPETITIVE EDGE

- Learn the secrets of the greatest public speakers in the world
- Influence others by mastering platform skills
- Learn the DOs and DON'Ts

WHO SHOULD ATTEND

Leaders and the potential leaders who are looking of gaining a competitive edge through public speaking.

Shiv Khera